AMERICAN EDUCATION

Its Men,

Ideas,

and

Institutions

Advisory Editor

Lawrence A. Cremin
Frederick A. P. Barnard Professor of Education
Teachers College, Columbia University

AMERICAN EDUCATION: *Its Men, Ideas, and Institutions* presents selected works of thought and scholarship that have long been out of print or otherwise unavailable. Inevitably, such works will include particular ideas and doctrines that have been outmoded or superseded by more recent research. Nevertheless, all retain their place in the literature, having influenced educational thought and practice in their own time and having provided the basis for subsequent scholarship.

GENERAL EDUCATION

in the

PROGRESSIVE COLLEGE

By

Louis T. Benezet, Ph.D.

ARNO PRESS & THE NEW YORK TIMES

*New York * 1971*

Reprint Edition 1971 by Arno Press Inc.

Reprinted from a copy in
  The University of Illinois Library

American Education:
  Its Men, Ideas, and Institutions - Series II
ISBN for complete set: 0-405-03600-0
See last pages of this volume for titles.

Manufactured in the United States of America

Library of Congress Cataloging in Publication Data

Bénézet, Louis Tomlinson, 1915-
    General education in the progressive college.
    (Teachers College, Columbia University.
Contributions to education, no. 884) (American
education: its men, ideas, and institutions.
Series II)
    Originally presented as the author's thesis,
Columbia, 1943.
    Includes bibliographical references.
    1. Education, Higher--U. S. I. Title.
II. Series: Columbia University. Teachers
College. Contributions to education, no. 884.
III. Series: American education: its men,
ideas, and institutions. Series II.
LB2322.B4 1971   378.73   70-165704
ISBN 0-405-03693-0

GENERAL EDUCATION

in the

PROGRESSIVE COLLEGE

By

Louis T. Benezet, Ph.D.

Associate Professor of Psychology,
Knox College

TEACHERS COLLEGE, COLUMBIA UNIVERSITY

CONTRIBUTIONS TO EDUCATION, NO. 884

Bureau of Publications

TEACHERS COLLEGE, COLUMBIA UNIVERSITY

NEW YORK, 1943

To my wife
MILDRED T. BENEZET
this joint work is affectionately dedicated

Foreword

THE experimental college—that institution which dedicates itself as a whole to an adventure in new ideas for higher education—is not new in America. Thomas Jefferson founded the University of Virginia to pioneer in the broadening of offerings for the college student of 1820. Andrew White at Cornell carried on the same kind of broadening experiments later in the century. In the sixties, Charles W. Eliot gave the free elective system carte blanche in the Harvard curriculum; and fifty years later, the principle was still fresh enough to provide a key feature for the first twentieth century experimental college, Reed.

In the decade following the first World War, experimental education in the grades and high school spread faster than it did in the colleges. In fact, the eventual "experimental colleges" of that era were frankly eager to borrow new ideas from the lower grades. As a result of such honest borrowings, these colleges came to be called "progressive colleges," in tune with the contemporary "progressive schools" and their sponsoring body, the Progressive Education Association (founded in 1918).

Throughout the nineteen thirties the new, "progressive colleges" played a conspicuous part in the advance of fundamental changes in higher education. Yet to date little has been written about the collective educational beliefs of these important contributors. This study, then, is one limited attempt to see a part of the ideas and practices of the so-called "progressive" college.

It should be made very clear at the outset that the institutions in the study are not the only ones which have become known as "progressive colleges"; they are but three of a group of five and probably more. They were chosen for their physical accessibility; or rather, others were left out mainly because they were too far away to be included in a program of personal visits on the campus. Thus the study of three, Sarah Lawrence, Bennington, and Bard, as examples of a generic "progressive college" is a hypothesis which stands or falls partly upon the extent to which Black Mountain, Rollins, possibly Reed, and others, will agree with the essential spirit of what is reported in this book. So far as the writer's own investigation has shown, the level of that basic sympathy runs safely high.

For help in making this study, thanks are due first to the administrations and staffs of Sarah Lawrence, Bennington, and Bard. Needless to say, without their active help the study could not have been made. From the first they have shown an intelligent interest in the problem. With complete cooperation in each case, the personnel, facilities, and records were made available to the visitor, plus a large amount of friendly hospitality thrown in. The data volunteered on all sides, moreover, came to include much that could not be squeezed between the covers of one small study. For this, added thanks, and apologies, must go to several officers, notably the Director of Education at Sarah Lawrence, the Director of Student Personnel at Bennington, the Registrar of Bard, and the Librarians of the three Colleges. Ex-President Robert D. Leigh of Bennington, in informal personal conference, gave invaluable suggestions leading to the original formulation of the study problem.

For basic aid from start to finish, thanks are inadequately given to my friend and sponsor, Donald P. Cottrell, whose genius for crystalizing tough verbal problems was often put to the test. Wise advice at frequent stages was granted by Professors Floyd B. O'Rear, R. Freeman Butts, and Donald G. Tewksbury. Unpublished documents from their personal files were lent, along with friendly advice, by Dr. William H. Kilpatrick; Dr. Caroline B. Zachry; and Dr. Joseph O. Chassell. For helping shape the thinking with which the underlying problems were approached, a large personal debt is felt to Harold Rugg, who by his active faith in an enlightened future for democracy surely has helped to embody the progressive spirit in American education.

L.T.B.

September, 1942

Contents

Chapter I

Introduction: Aims and Methods in College Education

IN THE confusion that marks discussions and writings about college education today one thing seems clear: the spirit of status quo, even in our most conservative institutions, is no more. Its disappearance, whether permanent or temporary, might perhaps be laid to the growing recognition on all sides of a feeling something like that expressed by one renowned teacher, Irwin Edman, in *Philosopher's Holiday*:

> There is only one thing by which I continue, with a foolish and persistent naivete, to be surprised. I expect, somehow, that a student ten years after college will still have the brightness and enthusiasm, the disinterested love of ideas, and the impersonal passion for them that some develop during their undergraduate days. Time and again I have run into them, and wondered what the world had done to them that that passionate detachment should have gone. I know some of the things, brutal or familiar enough almost to the point of banality: a family, the struggle for a living, a disillusion with the status of contemplation in the nightmare of a violent world. But it is not revolution or disillusion that surprises me; both are intelligible. It is the death-in-life that assails the spirits of young men who had been alive when I knew them at college. . . . It is when spirit is utterly dead, when the one-time eager youth becomes precociously middle-aged, that one feels above all that education is a failure. . . .[1]

Such a criticism, to be sure, inclines toward the literary. It might, also, be argued that Professor Edman is flaying not so much the educational system as human nature, and the kind of life men have to live after leaving college. The crucial fact remains, however, that teachers and laymen alike in America

[1] p. 122. 1938. Quoted by permission of Viking Press, publishers.

1

tend to share his belief, that college education does not suffi-
cently "stick."

Evidence confirming this is too well known to demand large
space in any contemporary educational discussion. On the professional critic's side, the tirades of Hutchins against "body-
building, character-building, the social graces, and the tricks
of trades" have become conventional openings as thesis or an-
tithesis in higher educational debate, joining the intellectualist
tradition of Presidents Day and Porter of Yale, Cardinal New-
man, Dean West of Princeton, Flexner, Foerster, and many
more. On the semi-objective and popular level stands John R.
Tunis's *Was College Worthwhile?*, in which he concludes,
"The lamp of learning—handed down to us in a direct line
through Paris, Oxford, and Cambridge, has at last produced a
group of men whose chief ambitions, if their record tells the
truth, is to vote the Republican ticket, to keep out of the
bread line, and to break 100 at golf. . . . does one need to go
to college to have such aspirations?" [2]

Even if the first criticism quoted should provoke more argument than agreement, and the second, no more than wry smiles,
the widely-known report by The Carnegie Foundation for the
Advancement of Teaching on "The Study of the Relations of
Secondary and Higher Education in Pennsylvania" lends an
authority which will hardly bear question. A review of some of
its more startling findings, four years after their first issue, may
still be provocative:

On the series of objective tests of "General Culture" (combined
scores in General Science, Foreign Literature, Fine Arts, and Social
Studies), 28.4% of the college seniors did less well than the average
sophomore, and nearly ten per cent did less well than the *average
high school senior.*

22% of the high school senior scores surpassed the average college
sophomore level.

15% of the college seniors made either the same scores as, or lower
scores than, they had made as sophomores.

[2] p. 234. 1936.

On a series of tests in Mathematics, English, Social Studies, Fine Arts, Science and Literature, 12% or about one-eighth of over a thousand high school seniors scored *above the mid-point* of the scores of college seniors expecting to teach.[3]

These findings, it must be said, do not pay justice to many individuals and colleges making excellent scores. Granting that, what was wrong with the others? Or why, in general, do students, teachers, alumni, as well as outsiders, tend to believe that college education does not stick?

The present state of higher educational aims—that is, the formulation of what the college is consciously trying to do—may furnish one answer. The methods and materials it is using toward the accomplishment of those aims may offer another answer. *The kind of relation which exists between what the college is trying to do and what methods and materials it is using* should provide a crucially important third answer—if "answer" it may be called. As the supposed meeting place of the other two, this last also may offer a central point of focus for a study of how the college of today is attempting to meet some of the problems that it faces.

In the building of a house, any architect will tell us, there is a Siamese-twin relationship between the design for the eventual house and the kind of structural devices and materials which are available to carry out this design. A change in either side, such as a shortage of certain materials, predicates a fundamental change in the nature of the other side. This inseparable relation between idea and method in building-construction was expressed, for instance, by a great late nineteenth century architect, Louis H. Sullivan: [4] the form (or design, or idea) of anything is determined by *the function which it is to fulfill.*

Such simple architectural truths as the foregoing seem wise enough to hold applicability for all types of structure, whether

---

[3] W. S. Learned and Ben D. Wood, *The Student and His Knowledge.* 1938. Although this study was limited by the purpose to (p. 11) "examine that aspect of educational achievement for which trustworthy measures could be found, namely, the student's knowledge," such a limitation can hardly rule out the significance of the findings—no matter what other more subjective or personal values may accrue during college.

[4] In *The Autobiography of an Idea,* p. 290. 1924.

it be the building of a house or the organization of a college. Yet many American colleges fall considerably short of showing the same consistency. On the contrary, it is being increasingly realized in self-critical times like the present that: (1) college aims have typically been either inadequately conceived or unclearly stated; (2) that the methods adopted to fulfill these aims do not exemplify any such "Siamese-twin" relationship as was posited above to be a *sine qua non* for sound construction.

Relative to the first point, the late Dean Haggerty, after the exhaustive fifty-seven college survey by a Committee of the North Central Association of Colleges and Secondary Schools on *The Evaluation of Higher Institutions,* concluded: "Clearness of conception implies that the aims of an institution are expressed in a formal statement that is unequivocal. . . . In general, the pages of college catalogues leave much to be desired in these matters. . . ." [5] More recently, the already famous Eight Year Study by the Progressive Education Association's Commission on the Relation of School and College has revealed conditions leading the Director of the Study to report: "It must be said here that liberal arts college faculties seldom state clearly what they mean by liberal or general education. Perhaps they do not know. . . . Rarely . . . have whole college faculties cooperatively thought their problem through and set forth their purposes and plans." [6]

· On the second point, the relation of college methods to college aims, another quotation from Haggerty is helpful:

It does not necessarily follow that, because an institution accepts culture as an educational objective, its activities contribute to such an outcome. . . . One college registrar struck at the very heart of this matter when he complained after a new and elaborate set of objectives had been adopted that the new aims had altered the activities of the institution not a whit. *The reality of any aim is to be measured by the extent to which it results in a sequential chain of activities leading to its accomplishment. This is the crucial test of sincerity in educational thought and practice.*[7]

[5] M. E. Haggerty, *The Educational Program; The Evaluation of Higher Institutions,* Vol. III, p. 107. 1937.

[6] W. M. Aiken, *The Story of the Eight-Year Study,* pp. 119–120. 1942.

[7] Haggerty, *op. cit.,* p. 50. Italics mine.

Once again, a more recent survey of the field strongly hints that the colleges either have not yet seen fit or else have not yet found ways to fuse their practices with their ideas. Reporting for the American Council on Education's Committee on Student Personnel Work, on the subject of college education for social competence, Esther Lloyd-Jones writes: "Studies of the programs that colleges have developed thus far [586 college catalogs examined], . . . reveal few efforts that go beyond 'curriculum-tinkering' that are specifically designed to accomplish these purposes which colleges so eloquently avow." [8]

What has been discussed so far about the over-all scene takes on a sharper meaning when the focus is turned on the individual case. Let us look at parts of three or four college catalogues, selected for no special reason beyond the fact that they do state their colleges' educational aims—by no means a universal practice:

College 1 (men's) states, during its five pages of educational aims, "The uniqueness of each student must be honored." This is followed by the statement that fifteen units will be required for entrance, "drawn from the usual college preparatory subjects of English, mathematics, foreign language, science, and social studies." The Committee on Admissions does consider exceptions. Under courses of study, four years of public speaking are required of everybody, plus the conventional requirements of two years in science, one year in English composition, and a foreign language.

College 2 (coeducational) states ". . . the college holds as a primary responsibility the discovery of the individual student . . . his needs, interests and purposes. . . ." Yet its program sets rigid subject-matter requirements for admission, prescribes four courses in the freshman year, lists no individual study provisions other than a limited program (2 or 3 semester credits) of honors work in the major, and requires regular class and chapel attendance, and final examinations in every course which is taken for credit.

College 3 (women's) aims to "develop individuality," and

8 *Social Competence and College Students*, p. 6. 1940.

states as part of its purpose an emphasis on "the growth of the individual and the development of her social awareness." Yet, in its requirements for graduation, it holds to an ancient women's college tradition: "Students who do not present on entrance two units of Latin or Greek must take one year of Latin in college"—this being included in a solid page of general course, hour, and divisional requirements.

College 4 (coeducational) states, among its explicit aims, "Self-government is a feature of an educated man," and later, "The college seeks to keep abreast of the times." Then, in the section under General Information, one reads that the use of tobacco, though not forbidden, is "deprecated" and relegated to locations outside the college buildings and grounds, and that the mere evidence of use of alcoholic beverages is regarded as "sufficient ground for termination of an individual's connection with the institution."

The above review of non-sequiturs, revealing themselves to the most casual catalog-reader, might be amusing if they were not so typical of hundreds of others, or if they did not remind one of the jutting tip of the iceberg, which warns of nine-tenths of its bulk lying below. They serve as pointers, in other words, of a situation in the organization of the American college which may in truth be as serious as Haggerty evidently thought it to be when he wrote:

> In all of these matters most American colleges and universities appear to be below the level of quality that is desirable for the adequate care and cultivation of youth. The truth of this statement is attested by practically every factual study of higher education that has been made in recent years. It is supported by the inadequate performance of college graduates in the practical affairs of life. The time would seem to be at hand for institutional self-examination in order that the quality of education may be elevated.[9]

How true or false this rather gloomy picture is accepted to be depends upon the standard of expectancy held for anything so human and variable as a college. If by that standard the picture be judged true (as this discussion argues), it still does

[9] Haggerty, *op. cit.*, p. 7.

not follow immediately that American colleges, more or less deliberately, have rejected "the crucial test of sincerity" (see above, p. 4), in that they hold to practices which do not match their stated aims. This, nearly every college administrator in the country would earnestly deny. What seems a good deal more likely is that the task at present is simply too hard.

The design, methods, and materials for building a house, as have been used in illustration, are one matter; the design, methods, and materials of building a place to educate men and women for contemporary society are a different business. Their complexities and intangibles reveal themselves in the amazingly diverse and growing lists of books on college education written in this century, especially during the last twenty years. Most of these books amply show the difficulty of getting down to universal truths in this field. A few, such as the early *College Administration* by Thwing (1901) and *College and University Administration* by Lindsay and Holland (1930), have tried to generalize in some measure the problem and its details. For the great part, however, the writings tend to take form either as reports, direct or indirect, about specific institutions, or as detailed studies of some particular part of the college structure. The summary impression remains, that matching the aims and the methods of a college takes on reality only when seen in the light of a particular, local situation; and that even then it has not been very well solved anywhere.

The nearest approach to a single treatment of the college aims-methods question is Fraser's five hundred-page essay, *The College of the Future*.[10] As an almost unique example of its kind, it deserves some pause for review. The central assumption therein is stated to be that a college's educational fitness rests upon knowing "what, how, and whom to teach" (these Fraser considers mutually inseparable). The principal task within this area is held to be the selection of students who can learn, teachers who can teach, and curricular material which will permit, the building up of "inclusive aims" concerning the relation of the student to his society. The objective is the

[10] M. G. Fraser. 1937.

"greatest harmonious growth in the various phases of living." [11]
The methods to be stayed with throughout are those which
will seek out and build on the student's "genuine interests"
about himself, his work, and his world.

Such an effort as this to deal with the over-all aims that the
college should embrace in America today would seem to have
enough fundamental wisdom that it should hardly be absent
from any college president's working-library shelf. Yet, as Dr.
Fraser would probably be the first to point out, his philosophical opus gives no prescription to College X or College Y for the
solution of their particular aims-and-methods problems. It
does not attempt to show, for instance, how a curriculum giving adequate introduction to all the "various phases of living"
(Fraser names six major divisions of these) could be fitted to a
certain student who can "do" science and mathematics but who
simply has no verbal facility. It does not try to explain how
such a curriculum could be presented by a mediocre faculty,
not too well balanced academically. It does not give the president a formula by which he finds himself suddenly able to get
enough endowment for his college to achieve the "economic
independence from the great society" [12] which Fraser believes
is necessary for "sound and expeditious teaching in all the various phases of living." It is true that such a book as Fraser's refers directly to dozens of plans in use among colleges today,
and that it discusses fairly specifically such items as objective
tests, the cost of individual instruction, and the value of competitive athletics. Yet the fact remains that for the average college executive, the prime use of a philosophical work of this
kind probably will be to impress him with the profound implications in his job. It will show him rather less about how
to define aims suitable to his own particular college setting,
and how then to proceed with the material he has at hand.

In brief, what seems to be needed next is a study (as yet nowhere available) which takes up the large pattern for the college of the future as Fraser and others have outlined it, and

[11] p. 142.
[12] p. 108.

tries to show what this pattern comes to mean in terms of the business of educating human beings of college age, through the efforts of human beings variously older and more trained. Such a study might become possible through a collaboration of whatever efforts are needed (such as by psychologist, sociologist, and educationist) to bridge the gap between the philosopher's general prescription and the college educator's special problems that arise in trying to make that prescription work.

To bring this down to earth, there is apparent in the background of higher educational debate today a row of stumbling blocks which still manage to bark the shins of the best efforts toward vitalizing the college program. Mention of a few of these, in question form, may show the essential kinds of trouble involved:

Is there a body of facts about the world today essential enough that all college students should be expected to learn them?

If so, how can they be distinguished from other, "non-essential," facts?

If distinguishable, how can *all* the facts be "taught" to *all* students, in a lasting way?

If there is a distinguishable residue of facts to be learned by all college students today, how can a small college, with a limited staff, cover the teaching of all these facts?

How can a boy or girl with fairly special interests be induced to study with a real drive in *each one* of the "various phases of living"? Or is this to be held necessary?

In terms of human learning, what is the real distinction between "specialized" learning and "general" learning?

How can *social living*, in the small and large views, be effectively "taught" in college?

Granting the importance of certain "qualitative values" [13]

[13] President H. M. Wriston, in *The Nature of a Liberal College* (1937), proposes four principal ones: precision; appreciation; opinion; reflective synthesis.

(as being more important than "facts," beyond, perhaps, those considered above as essential), can such values be made measurable in the student's learning, and the teacher's teaching? If so, how?

To say that these questions are not being very successfully answered by the colleges is only an elaborated way of repeating once again the charge that colleges have not yet found methods adequate to their present aims. At the present time, no general study of the vitals of this relationship is available to help them. Traditionally, each college has worked out the matter by itself, for good or ill. This may be inevitable, in that the local and personal nature of such relationships make one central study of the problem impracticable. Unlike Fraser's proposal of a philosophical base for the college of the future, perhaps a general study of aims-methods questions, even if it could be achieved, would be of no special use to the individual college. (Certainly, it should be made clear at once, the report of the particular study to follow has no such omnibus intentions.) Yet, on many campuses today, the need for something of this sort remains.

The criticisms just presented have tended to be sweeping without making reference to which kinds of colleges might and which might not be examples in point. Needless to say, many colleges exist today whose methods and aims are in good, working harmony. These might be put into two broad classes. Only one of the classes should command any long concern here.

The first class comprises those colleges which have enjoyed an aims-method harmony simply by refusing to change either their aims *or* their methods since the institution was started. As the opening sentence in this chapter implies, theirs is a vanishing breed. They have prospered by appealing to virtues easily dispensed through the facilities of the school: the ability to read and write certain ancient and modern languages; command of mathematics, if kept unapplied; various degrees of familiarity with the physical and social world; a polite acquaintance with belles lettres; and, through it all, a cultivated respect for the picture held before them of a world ruled by the Liberal Arts—a world which, after they left those halls, they really were hardly expected to see again. Whether or not this kind of learning, when properly impelled, stuck, is an issue to be contested on pages other than these.[14] The fact remains that the trend has been away from the type of college which confines itself to such functions.[15] The majority-feeling today favors the conclusion that this type of college learning cannot and should not stick, because both its aims and its methods are foreign to the contemporary college boy's own aims and practices, and to the aims and practices of his society. Another kind, a subtler kind, of integration is needed in the college program today.

The second class of colleges which have reached a aims-method harmony (omitting for clarity's sake all the gradations between this and the first class) contains, at its best, that college which has set out deliberately to take its aims from as much of the contemporary scene as it feels it can handle, and then to pick methods suited to these aims. Its other distinguishing feature is, by necessity, that it has been founded for educational, not social or economic, reasons. The ideal picture therefore becomes a college whose aims and methods have been forged in one piece and tempered in the trends and needs of society today. Usually, such a college is realistic enough to claim a position somewhere short of this ideal.

This description may sound so vague that all colleges who are making any changes at all might claim membership to this "second class." Most of them will not bear up under inspection. Their kinds of reform too often reveal ironical non-sequiturs of the general order illustrated above (pp. 5–6). They reveal, also, a useful basis for distinguishing the college which does truly belong to this class from the one which does

---

[14] For an analogous, though not identical, argument, see R. M. Hutchins, *The Higher Learning in America* (1936) for the pro, and H. D. Gideonse, *The Higher Learning in a Democracy* (1937) for the con, regarding the strength of a "classical" education.

[15] Much of R. F. Butts's *The College Charts Its Course* (1939) centers on this point. See especially Chap. XXII, pp. 417–424.

not, namely, *the pervasiveness, within the college, of the changes made.* Unless the instituted reforms and new ideas embrace the activities of the college *as a whole,* non-sequiturs and compromises seem bound to remain.

This means that in order to achieve a harmony between the kinds of aims and methods which truly stem from the trends of the present day, the college must either reorganize itself from top to bottom,[16] or start as an entirely new college—campus, administration, staff, and all. The difficulties in the former course may be reflected in the fact that few real examples of such a process have started and managed to keep going [17] (although one such forms a third part of the study to follow). Examples of the latter—the truly "experimental" college—are yearly becoming more numerous. Although the struggle for existence among many of them is stern, in some cases fatal, they are giving far more than their share of momentum to progress in college education.

Under the title of "experimental colleges" these new ventures have been characterized, as a group, by Cottrell:

The experimental colleges, rather more than colleges generally, are self-conscious institutions. They not only share in the usual broad purpose to promote enlightenment but they have also formulated a body of fairly explicit principles for their own guidance. They have in considerable measure worked out the implications of their principles for a reasoned total outlook upon life and education. They seek to implement and advance some philosophy. This is not to say that there is a strict singleness of purpose in any one of these colleges, for frequently the groups are divided within themselves on many important points, but in their nature they have a basis of united action upon the experimental enterprise they seek to carry on.[18]

In the preceding pages it has been argued that no one general study exists, perhaps none can be made, of the complex

[16] Or, as a president was heard to say, "When you clean house, you have to do a good job of it."

[17] New College of Teachers College, Columbia University, and Dr. Meiklejohn's Experimental College of the University of Wisconsin are examples in point.

[18] D. P. Cottrell, in *General Education in the American College,* p. 194. 1939. For a useful list of criteria of the experimental college see also p. 195 of that study.

of problems which come from trying to match college educational methods with worth-while, up-to-date aims. If this remains true, a next best thing might be to examine the course of two or three of these new colleges which have consciously set out to take on that task. Such, in brief, is the purpose of the study to follow.

To examine the course of all the aims and all the methods of even two or three colleges would require time and authority well beyond that possible in the present case. In an attempt to cut the area down to size, therefore, a problem within the college curriculum was selected which might be small enough for an outsider to grasp during a reasonable period of study, and yet full enough of implications to reflect, in some reduced way, all that the colleges in question have to deal with, and the way in which they typically deal with it. The problem selected was *general education*. The report to follow considers, first, how general education is interpreted in various ways in the American college today; second, how the three "experimental" colleges selected have developed principal aims and methods during their short histories; third, how general education is viewed and presented at these colleges; and last, what lessons, if any, for over-all problems of curricular aims-and-methods in college education may be seen.

The three colleges selected for study, Sarah Lawrence, Bennington, and Bard, form a part of the group of young colleges which are making themselves known as testing-grounds for new ideas in college education. Respectively they are fourteen, ten, and eight years old (counting from date of actual opening). The first two, women's colleges, were established as new ventures, backed by private funds; Bard, a man's college, took over the campus, the holdings, part of the student body, about one-third of the staff, and the "dominion-status" under Columbia University, of St. Stephens, a seventy-year-old Episcopal College in Dutchess County, New York. The three colleges are, respectively, about twenty, two hundred, and one hundred miles north of New York City.

In their administration the three schools are similar in offering liberal arts programs to small bodies of students (*circa* 280, 290, and 150), and in operating by means of high tuition rather than large endowments. This permits them to maintain a high faculty-student ratio (varying between one to five and one to seven); but it means also, of course, that the clientele is preponderantly well-to-do. Scholarship and reduced-tuition plans somewhat broaden the range.

Chiefly (although this must be examined closely later on) they have come to be associated together because of two important and common planks in their educational platforms, which have greatly affected both their methods and their aims: (1) student responsibility and participation; and (2) individuation of student work. The recognition of these common faiths, whether conscious or unconscious, has been reflected in a good deal of friendly contact among the three schools, as well as several changes of staff members from one college to the other (including Bard's present Dean, formerly teacher at Bennington). More important to this study, the avowal of these faiths has earned for them the informal title, at least within their region, of "progressive colleges."

A concluding word in this introduction probably is needed to explain on what basis "progressive colleges" has been used, even in the title, to refer to these particular three colleges.

The most formidable-sounding questions in education sometimes have the simplest answers. Questions about the use of the term progressive, directed at four qualified people,[19] enabled the following answer to be evolved:

The chief criterion for a school or college's being called "progressive" is *the school's or college's own willingness to be known as such.* It usually implies a belief in educational principles sponsored by the Progressive Education Association, which in turn derived them from the teachings of forefront thinkers since the time of James and Dewey.[20] *These prin-*

[19] Dr. William H. Kilpatrick; Frederick L. Redefer, Director of the Progressive Education Association; James L. Hymes, Jr., then Editor of *Progressive Education;* Professor R. Freeman Butts, author of *The College Charts Its Course.*

[20] Stanwood Cobb (first President of P. E. A.): ". . . Professor Dewey, whose philosophy is the foundation and inspiration of educational reform in this country." In "The New Quarterly," *Progressive Education,* Vol. I, p. 4, April, 1924.

ciples, however, have nowhere been crystallized into a state-
ment of what, for instance, "progressive" schools or colleges
should or should not do to earn the title.

For its first five years, for example, the magazine *Progressive Education* ran a page on the reverse side of its table of contents entitled "The Principles of Progressive Education." [21] These were listed as (1) freedom to develop naturally; (2) interest, the motive of all work; (3) the teacher a guide, not a taskmaster; (4) scientific study of pupil development; (5) greater attention to all that affects the child's development; (6) cooperation between school and home to meet the needs of child life; (7) the Progressive School a leader in Educational Movements. In the first quarterly, 1929, these principles were somewhat revised, and the page was entitled simply "Progressive Education." In the May, 1930, issue, at the time of a change in P. E. A. presidents, the page was dropped and has not been resumed.

An attempt at last to state at least the working philosophy of progressive education was made by a chosen committee, working from 1938 to 1941, and the results eventually were published as a yearbook supplement in the magazine.[22] The article's content is not of direct concern here, beyond the opening sentences: "It is entirely normal that within the membership of the Progressive Education Association there should be wide differences of position and conviction. It is the essence of the progressive attitude that differences be carefully protected, even fostered." [23] To be progressive, then, need not mean any one set of things.

Meanwhile, the essential point already made—that being called progressive is at heart a matter of avowal, not definition —is made further clear in the statement at the heading of the magazine's monthly Educational Directory (columns of school advertisements):

[21] p. 2. 1924–1929.
[22] Harold Alberty, "Progressive Education—Its Philosophy and Challenge," *Progressive Education,* May, 1941.
[23] *Ibid.,* p. 3.

It would be undesirable, if not entirely impossible, to classify schools at present as progressive or otherwise. *Progressive Education* is glad, however, to bring before its readers for their investigation *schools which have signified their desire to carry out the principles of Progressive Education.* Only advertisements of such schools will be accepted by the magazine.

The same policy is used at the P.E.A. office, it has been advised, in replying to outside requests for the names of "progressive colleges." The natural outcome is that only those schools and colleges which, in the method and content of their teaching, embrace progressive principles as a whole are or might be willing to take on the name "progressive school" or "progressive college." This seems as it should be.[24]

In the case of Sarah Lawrence, Bennington, and Bard, orientation of the program as a whole to such principles as the Progressive Education Association promotes among elementary and secondary schools has been avowed. It has been freely mentioned by the heads of those colleges, and implied if not directly stated in their catalogs (this will be subject to inspection in Chapters III, IV, and V). It has led to natural feelings of mutuality between these colleges and the P.E.A., giving rise often to such professional contacts, conferences, etc., among the personnel as might be expected.

The result of this program orientation and these ties of feeling has been an un-self-conscious reference to the three colleges in question, from time to time, as progressive colleges.

[24] The points just given are surprisingly closely checked by the report of a luncheon conference of the Annual Meeting of the A.A.C., in Atlantic City, 1933 (President E. H. Wilkins of Oberlin, conference leader). The topic was "What Constitutes a Progressive College?" President Wilkins reports that "among the points of explicit or apparent agreement among the spokesmen of these (Sarah Lawrence, Bennington, and Rollins) colleges were: [presented here in abridged form] (1) a matter of *attitude* rather than particular devices; (2) a readiness to adapt the college to the "true and changing" needs of college students; (3) flexibility in the use of all instruments of college activity; (4) involves study of each student as an individual; (5) involves a heightened degree of faculty-student co-operation; (6) "recognition and development of those educational values inherent in what are usually called extra-curricular activities"; (7) "that the attitude in question, if it is to be effective, cannot be delegated and dismissed to special offices, but must permeate the entire faculty." *Bulletin of Association of American Colleges,* Vol. 19, pp. 108–109, March, 1933.

(There are others; it has been regretted, for instance, that Black Mountain could not be included in this study; Rollins likewise is generally thought kindred in spirit if somewhat less close in program.)

Following this lead, the present study will use "progressive college" to refer to Sarah Lawrence, Bennington, and Bard, not because they hew to the letter of some *ex cathedra* definition of the term, but because they have been willing to avow, in their aims and methods, beliefs and practices fundamentally akin to those of the progressive movement in twentieth century American education.

A final word of caution is compelled by the fact that Bennington in 1942 inaugurated program changes which will lead it, by intention, farther away from some of the actual methods of the other two colleges than has so far been the case. This may require, in some of the sections to follow, discussion of Sarah Lawrence, Bard, and Bennington-up-until-1942. The requirement is, perhaps, well imposed. It should serve as a needed reminder that what we are to study here is not a set of ideas in triplicate, but the courses of three separate colleges, making separate attempts to grapple with the problem of matching methods with aims in the college of and for today.

Chapter II

General Education in the American College

INTRODUCTION

COLLEGE education, according to the evidence in the introductory discussion, does not stay with the typical American graduate for very long. The impression from this might be that the colleges have not done much to try to change the situation. The opposite, of course, is strikingly true. During the last fifteen to twenty years proposals and reports of college reform have come virtually to deluge the educational scene.

A certain amount of argument over what should be the form and content of higher study has inevitably gone along with schools and scholars of history. The disputes about the Seven Liberal Arts versus "profane" Aristotelianism in the time of Abelard; Erasmus and Ramus's stumpings for humanism in the later Middle Ages; Ticknor's first pleas for "free" scholarship at Harvard in the 1820's [1]—all remind the student of college education that he is treading an ancient battlefield. Yet the systematic study by the college as a whole of the hows and whys of its program is a phenomenon of the present century, and more especially, the last twenty years.[2]

The professionalized approach to reviewing educational issues at one or many colleges was reported by W. C. Eells in 1937 (in *Surveys of American Higher Education*) formally to have begun in 1903. In that year the Mosely Commission came over from England to find out how American colleges and schools were managing to turn out the able engineers who had been reflecting

[1] See R. F. Butts, *The College Charts Its Course*, Chap. II. 1939.
[2] "College as a whole" may serve to distinguish the sort of activity implied from the work of individual pioneers of American college history in starting new plans: Thomas Jefferson at Virginia, Andrew White at Cornell, Eliot at Harvard, Harper at Chicago—to name a mere few.

their country's credit while working in the mines of South Africa.[3] Five years later saw two important studies launched: the Carnegie Corporation's survey of Medical Education, consummated by the now-historic report by Abraham Flexner; [4] and the first systematic college "self-study," carried out at Oberlin by a faculty committee.[5] Both studies inspired dozens of successors in the ensuing years, so that by 1937 Eells was able to work from a list of 579 documented American college surveys, including 233 that had been printed.

While the more or less formal "survey" has yielded perhaps the best body of comparable evidence on higher educational development, its progress seems slight when matched with the fabulous growth of new college "plans" of varying proportions, as reported in books and periodicals of recent years. Particularly since the first World War, colleges have demonstrated a spirit of "healthful discontent" [6] with themselves, though this discontent has actually been nothing more than the conscious or semiconscious reflection of the unmet demands placed upon them by an increasingly complex outside society.[7] One superficial way of gauging the result is merely to scan the entries in *The Education Index*, Volumes 1 to 4, under the heading, "Curriculum: Colleges and Universities." Volume I, 1929 to 1932, for instance, gives two columns of references to writings in this area (books and periodicals both included); Volume 4, 1938–41, gives more than five columns. That we are only now in the swell of it all is shown by the fact that the big jump— from two to five columns—takes place between Volume 2, 1932–35, and Volume 3, 1935–38. The titles listed cover every conceivable part of the program, from a new way to teach music to freshmen, to the problem of integrating the college

[3] Eells, *op. cit.*, p. 18.

[4] *Ibid.*, p. 29.

[5] *Ibid.*, p. 19.

[6] R. W. Ogan, "College Programs of Self Examination," *Journal of Higher Education*, Vol. XIII, p. 229, May, 1942.

[7] *Ibid.* Ogan lists five factors which contribute to college discontent: changing social conditions; varying enrollment, actual and prospective; conflicting educational philosophies; the accumulation of research evidence regarding human growth and development; and the persistent criticism of education (from outside).

experience as a whole. Successfully or not, colleges *are* acting creatively toward improving both methods and aims, in the face of the great needs of today.

In the early days of college surveys and new plans, it was customary to approach the educational program as a whole, and make the report of changes or need for changes on that basis. With the expansion of college education on the one hand, and the refinement of research methods on the other, the trend now is more toward working on one part of the program at a time. Although the omnibus kind of survey is still found, especially in reports and plans of new colleges, what Eells calls the shotgun type of study [8] has largely given way to an approach which carries a fairly definite idea of a particular area or problem to be examined. This sacrifice of breadth for depth, to be sure, has its drawbacks. The breaking-down and rebuilding-up of one small part of a curriculum may do more harm than good if, for instance, it neglects to plan a working relationship with the unchanged remainder—thus giving no basis for the necessary reintegration of the program as a whole.

Another recent trend in college study, though, may become of more and more use in offsetting such shortsightedness. Description of this trend can be quoted directly from Eells, based upon his digestion of opinions by thirty-six men most experienced in college survey work. They believe that the surveys of the future will be "not so microscopic in character as many that have been made. They will deal less with floor space, class size, and teacher load; they will go deeper into fundamentals and philosophy of the educational process; they will deal more with functions and processes, policies and programs, less with technicalities and the minutiae of organization. . . ." [9]

If the modern study in college education can thus manage to combine the cutting-down-to-size of the first trend with the going-down-to-fundamentals of the second, there seems some

[8] Eells, *op. cit.*, p. 243.
[9] *Ibid.*, p. 244.

reason to hope for results that really "mean business"—for the college or colleges concerned, and for the interested outsider as well. Such, perhaps, represents the best hope in the current study of a topic which is receiving a ground swell of attention today at the college (and also the secondary) level. This is the study of what, for great want of a better term, is called general education.

A first look at "general education" brings the impression that it is not a very good example of a problem cut down to size. For though admittedly a smaller topic than "education" or "college education," it does not at once present any more obvious handles by which to be grasped. This appears so true that the first conclusion about the subject almost inevitably becomes: there is no real agreement as to what "general" education is. To illustrate that fact, it is interesting to review three broad attempts within the past eight years (at the college level, where this discussion will stay) to make a collective study of the term and what it concerns.

In 1934 the Institute for Administrative Officers of Higher Institutions (organized in 1926) met at the University of Chicago and chose as its central theme, "A New Definition of General Education." What happened to this idea is stated in the preface of the eventual printed report of the meeting:

It was hoped . . . that one or more new definitions of general education might be proposed. Subsequent changes in the program eliminated this possibility. A review of the reports and discussions presented at the Institute led to the decision to adopt as the title for the Proceedings *General Education: Its Nature, Scope, and Essential Elements.*[10]

The wisdom of this change is eloquently supported by the body of the printed report, both by its range of conflicting opinions and by the very vague impression left with the reader as to just what even the "nature, scope, and essential elements" of general education have been shown to be.

An even larger attack on the problem makes up the Thirty-

[10] W. S. Gray (edr.), *General Education: Its Nature, Scope, and Essential Elements,* p. v. 1934.

Eighth Yearbook of the National Society for the Study of Education, Part 2, entitled *General Education in the American College*.[11] This book, a collection of sixteen articles by prominent educators, on every conceivable aspect of the topic, does not try to define general education beyond giving an outside conclusion at the start, by Alvin C. Eurich, the Chairman, and repeating it in the last chapter: "Clearly, it [general education] is an expression of a quest for unity and a renewed emphasis upon the democratic ideal."[12] The reports forming the body of the book, with the exception of one to be mentioned, apparently are glad to escape the definitive chore; for any guess as to their positions on the matter must be drawn by inference from the facts about college operations which they present.

In Chapter IX of this same yearbook, John Dale Russell adds crucial proof of the elusiveness of the central term. Twenty-two out of thirty-five liberal arts colleges which he solicited sent him their definitions of general education. After citing trends and disputes for several pages, Russell says, "We can hardly avoid the conclusion that confusion pervades the minds of many of those who discuss the subject."[13] His own attempt to present the majority opinion of those asked ends with this rather amazing clincher:

"Vocational education" is more amenable to definition. It refers to those educational processes which have a direct utility for a future career. . . . It refers to those procedures designed to develop skills, both mental and physical in character. *All else is general education.*[14]

The third collaborative approach to general education as a focus for study is still going on. Sponsored by the American Council on Education, and called the "Cooperative Study in General Education" (Ralph W. Tyler, University of Chicago, Chairman), it has brought together the attention of twenty-one higher institutions toward four working aims, the first of which is to assist faculties in redefining the aims of a program of

[11] G. M. Whipple (edr.). 1939.
[12] *Ibid.*, p. 13.
[13, 14] *Ibid.*, p. 183. Italics mine.

general education. For the discussion here the chief point of interest is to note that this study, like the others, consciously avoids what begins to sound like something of an academician's curse, the proposal of one definition for general education. In announcing the start of the study, E. J. McGrath makes that clear by saying that the committee would not be prepared "to accept any of the current definitions of general education as of universal validity." [15]

Again we are faced, in other words, with a picture which might be ludicrous if it were not a far from unique situation: three large official concentrations of reports and discussions, telling how general education is met and solved on various campuses and in various fields, but nowhere settling upon a decision as to what general education means. As has been shown, educators are aware of the paradox, and apparently believe it is not fatal. Although one may suspect *post hoc* reasoning, they point out that general education, like personality or democracy or electricity, is something which does not have to be basically defined to be worked with. Indeed, the fact that almost every college has its own definition (usually, likewise, derived *post hoc* from its plan of operations) is hailed as a wise recognition of uniqueness and democracy in the college educational set-up itself.

Yet for a study which aims to center its work in the area of general education it can hardly be enough to dismiss the meaning of the term upon such short and distant introduction. Granting the probability that it has not been and will not soon be defined to universal agreement in the American colleges, there are, as all the aforementioned studies go to prove, certain facts about general education that should be rehearsed before any meaningful discussion can go on. Logical definitions come hard in an area so ruled by operational factors as is a college curricular program. There are, however, other ways of defining such areas, which may gain in empirical truth what they lack in logical underpinnings. Specifically, general edu-

[15] "The Cooperative Study in General Education," *Junior College Journal*, Vol. 9, p. 500, May, 1939.

cation may come to be better understood through (1) a brief review of its rise into prominence on the college scene; (2) a look at what else there is in education with which it can be compared or contrasted (e.g. Russell's conclusion, p. 22); (3) the operational approach: that is, a summary of typical *working aims and programs* in "general education" in the colleges today, with inferences, when possible, about what thinking lies behind them. The last is by far the most common approach, is probably the most helpful, and will occupy most of the remaining space in this chapter.

APPROACHES TO THE MEANING OF GENERAL EDUCATION

Just when "general education" first appeared as a term to distinguish a definite part of the college program is not easy to discover. Loosely used, it can be found in such relatively early college critiques as Alexander Meiklejohn's *The Liberal College* (1920), when, in arguing for a Junior division in the four-year college, the author concludes: "If successful it (the Junior College) would make the concept of general liberal education a definite one." [16] Ten years later, in the compendium *Higher Education in America,* President Wilkins of Oberlin shows the casual way in which the term could then be employed: "College education should, therefore, be in part general, in part special . . . in part extensive, in part intensive." [17] That this casual type of reference was the rule during that period is further shown by the almost complete absence of talk about "general education" in an exhaustive report, two years later, of college experiments throughout America at that time. This book, *Changes and Experiments in Liberal-Arts Education,*[18] lists no plans especially designated as "plans for general education"; in fact, the words occur only five or six times, usually during offhand discussion, in the whole report.

[16] p. 158.
[17] R. A. Kent (edr.), p. 441. 1930.
[18] National Society for the Study of Education, *Thirty-first Yearbook,* Part 2, ed. by Guy M. Whipple. 1932.

When it is noted, moreover, that specific references to general education in the college curriculum do not appear in *The Education Index* until the 1935-to-1938 volume, the inference seems clear that, whatever the backgrounds, its rise to its present self-conscious importance in the college program is the product of very recent times.

What, then, caused the rise? To answer that would require a large task of separate research, at present not made. From the tentative opinions available,[19] the following, however, seems fairly clear:

The rise of attention to general education in college is an outgrowth of the expansion of student bodies in the 1920's and the early years of the depression. Vast numbers of boys and girls, unable to find jobs, and prompted in any case by a desire to extend their learning, went on to college after high school. That they did not know just what they wanted is probably a twin truth with the fact that the colleges did not know —and still don't—just what to give them. Both sides agreed on two points: it was not to be just a specialized training in one thing; and it was not to be just for the purpose of learning how to make a living. It was to be a "general" education.[20] Interpreting this very open order in terms of local needs, local facilities, and local ideas, the colleges went to work to provide "plans" for general education. In some cases these plans amounted mainly to pointing up certain features of the existing program which were felt to have this "general" value (such as Columbia's Contemporary Civilization course, and its many counterparts in other colleges). In other cases an entirely new entity was set up to handle the demand: witness Meiklejohn's Experimental College at Wisconsin (1927–1931), and the General Colleges of Minnesota (1932) and Florida (1935). In most cases, course offerings and requirements were juggled around

[19] See Eurich (pp. 3–14), and MacLean, Little and Works (pp. 135–137), both in *General Education in the American College*, 1939; and S. Scroggs, "Some Factors in General Education," *Journal of Higher Education*, Vol. X, pp. 147–152, March, 1939.

[20] It is interesting to note how this discussion comes out at a point almost exactly that of Russell's conclusion about what is and what is not general education (p. 24).

to insure the kind of program-spread that was believed to be the apotheosis of a general learning experience. In a few cases college officers declared they would continue to do what they had been doing all along, and merely do it better. Interspersed through this period of change, studies and conferences like those mentioned above helped to crystallize growing consciousness of the problem; and general education emerged from it all as a major issue in the college of today.

Another way of approaching what general education means is to see its use in discussion; that is, to watch for synonyms, antonyms, and comparisons which educators are wont to employ in its connection. This course may often lead to perplexing contradictions; but for the purpose here it is somewhat enlightening.

Viewing the term at the outset, H. M. Wriston, in the first chapter of *General Education: Its Nature, Scope, and Essential Elements,* pointed out [21] an initial source of confusion in the double reference of "general." "General," he noted, may refer either to "education which is made available to all"—that is, general in the sense that everybody "takes" it—; or it may refer to "the nature of the education provided"—that is, a quality or set of qualities which we seek to have in our educational program. The former meaning offers fairly slight relevance in this day; there is little argument found among colleges against the belief that, whatever the values of general education may be, it should be made general to all. Even professional and technical schools have come to accept this view.[22] It is the second meaning, the qualitative one, which is of central concern here.

General education is *not* education concerned directly with the individual's preparing for a particular means of getting a living: that much has been pretty well agreed upon. Yet this could not properly rule out the general values from the *experience of working,* or from learning about the world of work or

[21] Gray, *op. cit.,* p. 1.
[22] Earl J. McGrath and others, *General Education in the American College,* pp. 219–256. 1939.

about various vocational choices open to the individual today
—for these are widely held to have educative virtues beyond the
range of mere livelihood, and they form an important part of
several notable plans of general education (e.g., Minnesota,
Stephens, Antioch). If the mere-livelihood definition of vocational education is strictly held to, we have one antonym for
general education. But the borderline, it can be seen, is a
rather thin and shaky one.

On the synonym-side, there is apparent throughout the literature a persistent mushiness in the distinctions between general education and liberal education. Meiklejohn in 1920, it
has been shown above, simply lined the two together, imply-
ing that they help each other build a single concept. This belief was checked by Russell in his investigation of general education in the liberal arts college in the N.S.S.E. 38th Yearbook.
He reports [23] that the opinions on this point of the colleges solicited ranged from asserting that "liberal" and "general" are
synonymous, through various qualifications of this to the view
that liberal education is the greatest component of general
education, but that vocational and professional subjects also
contribute to general education.

H. M. Wriston, now President of Brown, himself has indi-
rectly added to the confusion in an interesting way. In the
same chapter of the 1934 volume *General Education: Its Nature, Scope, and Essential Elements,* mentioned above, he selects as "basic disciplines" for *general* education, precision,
appreciation, hypothesis, and reflective synthesis. In his 1937
work, *The Nature of a Liberal College,* he uses these same "disciplines," with one change of wording, as the essential virtues
of *liberal* education.[24]

The foregoing may serve to complete the indication that any
attempt to understand so vague a term as general education by

[23] N.S.S.E., *op. cit.* p. 177.
[24] The inference, needless to say, is not that President Wriston has been borrowing unknowingly from himself. Doubtless he would cast out the issue as ir-
relevant to what to him is the really important thing: the search for educational
principles which are of "universal validity."

appealing to another loosely used term is self-defeating and probably a waste of time. To clear up the discussion on "general" vs. "liberal" for the purpose of this study, which after all has committed itself to aims and methods, not definitions, in college education, it seems best to use "liberal education" in the baldest operational sense: that is, as "that kind of education which a liberal arts college program provides." General education from the same standpoint, then, becomes something which is provided, or attempted, at some point within that liberal arts program (as it happens, almost always in the first two years).

Reviewing other words frequently used in place of or alongside "general" education hardly offers more promise than the "liberal" education tangle. Briefly, the two most often found are "broad" and "cultural." The former seems clear enough and, in fact, is probably the nearest that general education has come to acquiring a fairly understandable dimension. The "cultural" still causes some misinterpretation, chiefly by its calling up in literal minds the old aristocratic conception of "the education of a gentleman" which has distinguished certain Eastern colleges of the past and, in a few residual centers, the present. Used more correctly to refer to *education for the culture,* it can help to point out one important direction for the general education programs to follow.

A summary of the discussion up to this point should, therefore, review the fact that general education came into the college program to give a vastly increased enrollment of unspecialized students some extension of their high school learning; that it has been variously designed to cover almost anything except specialized and vocational training; and that it is variously believed to be most effective when allied with liberal-education values, when it is broad in scope or implication, and when it is somehow related to the culture in which learners, teachers, and their college live. Beyond this, the confusion in definitions of general education points toward the wisdom of carrying any further study of the question into the third channel of approach: the field of operations actually going on at the present time.[25]

Viewed operationally, the definition of general education is approached in the colleges today via two major types of changes which may be roughly called the administrative and the curricular. Such a division to a large extent is futile, since an administrative change must have curricular implications, and no real curricular change can start until the administrative set-up makes it possible. Yet for the purpose of reviewing the situation, some distinction may be workable. Seen here, it is the distinction between the "extrinsic" and the "intrinsic" approach [26] to changes in the college program.

The predominantly administrative type of change is represented in the decision at many colleges that, whatever else it may be, general education is something that takes place in high school and the first two college years, ending when the student goes into his junior year of college. This view, presumably inspired by the European university tradition, is paralleled by the time-worn belief that the college student should know something about a lot of things (first two years) and achieve a thorough grasp of one (last two years). The resulting administrative change involves a splitting of the four years into a Lower Division (or Junior Division or Junior College), and an Upper Division. This practice even ten years ago had grown to such an extent that Kelly and Anderson were able to report [27] that 136 out of 676 higher institutions were using a curriculum organization more or less formally of this kind.

That this type of change revolves about the question of gen-

[25] The retreat from an attempt to define general education is temporary. Some further attempts to look definitively at the term will be made in Chapter VIII.

[26] See M. G. Fraser, *The College of the Future*, for the use of these words in connection with the college's educational program.

[27] R. L. Kelly and R. E. Anderson, "The Extent of the Divisional Development of the Curriculum," *Bulletin of the Association of American Colleges*, Vol. xix, pp. 418–424, December, 1933.

eral education is a truth revealed this year at the University of Chicago, where the separation of junior and senior division, under William Rainey Harper, originated fifty years ago. The decision there to award the B.A. degree after two years is explained by President Hutchins:

> It should be observed that the new bachelor's degree is not a "two year" degree. It is a degree given in recognition of general education. The curriculum will require the equivalent of four years, beginning with the junior year in high school.[28]

Administrative changes like this one are dramatic, and have the effect of precipitating gathered trends of new thinking. Yet they do not by themselves make clear what those trends of thinking are. Although the temptation is presented here to pause and guess at what definition of general education has led to the conclusion that it is something officially separable from the latter two years of college, the mere fact of such a large-scale, quantitative change by a college administration can hardly give enough evidence for an answer.

In a most real sense, the thinking of a college or a group of colleges on a problem like general education can be shown only by the specific curricular plans they devise to meet the problem, together with the reasons they give for their devices. Accordingly, the rest of the chapter presents a review of the most characteristic of these plans. First, however, a former method of inquiry (see Chapter I) is recalled. In order to focus what the plans are working *toward*, and in this way to continue efforts to clear up the meaning of "general education," it should be asked, on what *chief working aims*, if any, do all or most of the college plans agree?

Journeying along the miles of words said by colleges about their plans reveals at length a diversity of aims similar to (if not coincidental with) the confusion in definitions of general education mentioned above. There is, however, a concentration of agreement upon two large foci for those aims. These are worthy of some pause for study:

[28] R. M. Hutchins, "Hutchins Urges Degree Revision," *The New York Times*, Sec. 2, p. 5, Sunday, March 1, 1942.

1. Most statements of college aims for their programs of general education center about the democratic belief in *the primacy of the individual and his development*.[29] This is found by the colleges either in quantitive or in qualitative terms, sometimes in both.

By *quantitative* aims is meant the individual development through learning a lot of different things. As to what the range and precise nature of these things are, any widespread agreement is hard to find. The compromise usually reached is that they are contained somewhere in some kind of coverage of "the major fields of knowledge." This view, for instance, embraces all of the North Central Association's working definition of general education, as put forth in its "Manual of Accrediting Procedures":

> By general education is meant that type of education which acquaints a student with the facts and modes of thought in the chief fields of knowledge, such as natural science, literature, history and other social sciences, languages, and the fine arts, without the intent to fit him for any vocation in particular.[30]

On the *qualitative* side, the aims for individual development through general education take on virtues more like the "basic liberal disciplines" of Wriston, already discussed. The criterion becomes not what things the student has learned, but *what has happened to him* meanwhile. Modern educational and personality psychology in the past few years have shown that much in individual growth cannot be measured by tests of objective knowledge, and that the educational program must somehow officially recognize the student as "a unified, yet dynamic pattern of traits, abilities, skills, interests, and motivations, a bundle of teeming emotions, desires, and wants, dreams and passions." [31] In his analytical review of general education

[29] Educational Policies Commission, *The Purposes of Education in American Democracy*. 1938. First is listed "The objectives of self-realization." Walt Whitman is then quoted (p. 51): "The purpose of democracy . . . is . . . to illustrate, at all hazards, this doctrine or theory that man, properly trained in sanest, highest freedom, may and must become a law, and series of laws, unto himself."

[30] North Central Association of Colleges and Secondary Schools. (mimeographed.) p. 16.

[31] N.S.S.E., *General Education in the American College*, p. 353.

in the college today, one writer sums up the view of the person
who takes this attitude:

> In general education we use subject matter not so much as an end
> in itself but as an integrative and adjustive agent, as a means whereby
> the student can become aware of his thought processes and master
> the procedures of patterns of mental action.[32]

It is easy from this to see that what start out to be working
aims in the area of individual development, especially on the
qualitative side, become wordy and difficult as educators try to
grasp what this actually means in terms of human individuals,
and curricular plans. Yet the individual and his needs remains
as one main goal of the general education program, to the
agreement of virtually all. This goal, however, no longer
stands alone.

2. That education as a whole in the last fifteen years has
consciously taken on *society-centered aims* is a truth so profound that it is accepted on many sides as *the* trend of education in the present day. The dual pestilence of depression and
war during that time has moved the country to call upon education for unprecedented contributions to solidarity and social
welfare, whether it be assigning sugar-ration cards or instilling
loyalty to the principles of democracy. Educators themselves
for the most part have been quick to take up the call. The
summary position is typically stated:

> In brief, this choice means that education will come to grips . . .
> with the critical problems affecting the welfare of the people in our
> time in all areas of life—economic, political, social, moral, and in-
> tellectual. . . . The curriculum must be centered on the problems
> of our time.[33]

As might be expected, higher education's share in this has
mounted all out of proportion to the numbers it directly affects. This is due in part perhaps to the debt colleges and universities perennially owe to public and private benefaction.
That the return on the debt should take form in direct serv-

[32] Scroggs, *op. cit.*, p. 151.
[33] J. H. Newlon, *Education for Democracy in Our Time*, p. 224. 1939.

ice to the community was argued as early as 1904 by President Van Hise of Wisconsin,[34] and roundly affirmed by the late Lotus D. Coffman of Minnesota in his book, *The State University: Its Work and Its Problems.*[35]

Beyond these views of direct debt repayment, however, lies the persistent and widespread faith that out of the colleges will come those who in time can lead the world from darkness. Expressed by Herbert Hoover, in his "Resume" of the fifty-year celebration conference at Stanford University in 1941, this faith sounds strong and basic:

The universities can give guidance to constructive forces in time of crisis and they can check destructive forces. . . . The universities should sit in judgment upon those who claim the need of war . . . they can expose the aggressor; they can expose provocative action; they can hold up truth against propaganda; they can allay fear; they can call to a people to stop, look, and listen. . . .[36]

The universities (and colleges), though by now somewhat used to those fervent appeals which come during especially bad times outside, have by and large adjusted their aims and programs in the earnest attempt to suit society's demands. A look at any list of college curricular changes since America's entry into the present war, for instance, will reveal an almost endless array of plans to assist in the nation's short-term and long-term efforts. Writing more than a year before this time, R. L. Kelly in *The American Colleges and the Social Order* sums up the contemporary spirit: "In a word, there is an enlarged sense of responsibility for men and women of scholarship and wisdom to contribute to the public welfare."[37]

With the attention of the college so greatly turned toward the needs of society, inevitably the working aims for general

[34] "In the university men are trained to regard economic and social questions as problems to be investigated by the inductive method, and in their solutions to aim at what is best for the whole people rather than at what is favorable to the interests with which they chance to be connected." C. R. Van Hise, *Inaugural Address at the University of Wisconsin*, p. 20. 1904.

[35] 1934.

[36] Leland Stanford Junior University, *The University and the Future of America*, p. 271.

[37] p. 321. 1940.

education take on this same flavor. College catalogues now
follow up the dedications of their programs to the individual's
needs by pledging the direction of that individual toward the
tantamount needs of society.[38] Some of this, it is true, is chan-
neled into the student's major work in junior and senior year,
for traditional reasons expressed by Wilkins of Oberlin sometime ago: "If the man is to render efficient individual service
in the maintenance and development of human society he
must have a large measure of significant and ordered knowledge within some special field." [39] More and more, however,
the society-oriented aim is finding place in the goals stated for
the unspecialized part of the program: that is, in most cases, the
first two years.

Society-centered working aims, like the individual-centered
aims, are found in college statements to have both quantitative and qualitative aspects. On the former side, the aim is
given for the student to come to understand the major facts
and principles about human society today, and in particular,
about our own national culture. Again, what these major facts
and principles are deemed to be is found subject to a great deal
of variation.

On the qualitative side, on the other hand, the aims of the
general education program are usually expressed to be to bring
about a growth in the student's "social graces" and consideration of others, on the immediate scene; and the development
of a society-minded outlook, on the large scene. These aims are
subtle and difficult. Some colleges confess they are too subtle to
be attempted in the instructional program, and turn them over
instead to the personnel administration. Others contend that
the *right kind* of teaching on the quantitative side (i.e., the
facts and principles about society) will bring about all the cultural loyalties that could be desired. Fraser, for instance, in
The College of the Future,[40] writes his belief that colleges can
obtain the results wanted, and obtain them without fear of

[38] *Whittier College Bulletin, 1941–42,* for instance, divides its aims into
"Preparation for Living" and "Preparation for Service."
[39] Kent, *op. cit.,* p. 441.
[40] Fraser, *op. cit.,* p. 262.

being charged with "indoctrination," if they will teach so that the individual sees that his own "inclusive aims" must be co-extensive with the aims of society.

To summarize the working aims of general education in the college today, they are found to center about two foci: *the development of the individual and all his powers;* and *the orientation of that individual toward contemporary society and its needs.* Toward each focus two main methods of attack are used: the "quantitative," or fact-giving; and the "qualitative," or attitude-building.

Although it has not so far been mentioned, it can be rather quickly seen that discovering and putting side by side individual-centered and society-centered aims no more than begins the problem. Out of this duality must come *one plan,* to be directed, in the last analysis, at one individual. To reconcile the two centers of aims, and to build upon them a plan of general education which will have an integrative instead of a dispersive effect, is a task which colleges admit is as great as it is yet basically unsolved.

What then has come of the current attempts to build such a program? A description of six prevailing types in the American College will conclude this chapter.[41]

Division-sampling plans.

By far the most commonly used "plan" in the first two years of the American college starts by grouping subjects into large fields or divisions, and by then requiring the student by the

[41] Any attempts to describe a plan as representing a "type" are made only in conscious recognition that all typologies are dangerous and to an extent unreal. Large-scale overlapping and exceptions are the rule, in an area so diversely organized as a country-full of college plans.

N.B. The plans to be described center in the *selection of subject-matter*—i.e., the building of a curriculum—and are therefore not concerned with problems primarily administrative or personnel. This limitation must rule out separate consideration of the Junior College in America—a study all in itself—or of the guidance program (as an important catalyst in general education) *per se.* Lastly, reference will be held primarily to the liberal-arts type of college.

For an interesting example of the administrative type of program change, see K. I. Brown, *A Campus Decade,* 1940, a description of the Intensive Study Plan at Hiram College.

end of his sophomore year to have taken a prescribed number of courses in each "division." This system bases its case upon the belief that there do exist such large, internally-related fields of subject matter; that general education implies some knowledge of each field (see the North Central Association's definition of general education, above); and that taking one or two courses within each large field can give the student the essential discipline of that field as a whole.

The sampling method in the present day is usually backed up by a divisional rather than departmental organization of subject-fields.[42] Decision as to just what these divisions logically are is found to vary greatly. While Social Science and Natural Science as two are fairly universally accepted,[43] the remaining divisions may be one: e.g. Humanities, or Letters and Arts (Whitman College); two: e.g. Languages and Literature and Fine Arts [44] (Western College); or even three: e.g. Literature; Fine Arts; and Philosophy, Psychology, and Education (Reed College).

Whatever the local decision on these matters, the system which typically ensues is illustrated by the following pronouncement:

In order that every graduate shall have an introduction to each of the great fields of knowledge every student is required to complete fourteen hours in each of the three divisions of the curriculum. . . .[45]

In colleges where the departmental rather than divisional set-up is retained, such required distribution is usually determined by more or less traditional ideas of what should go into a liberal education. The form, in other words, follows the re-

[42] A sample of eleven college catalogs, for instance, revealed eight of these with divisional set-ups.

[43] Though not at Chicago, where the four divisions are Biological Sciences, Humanities, Physical Sciences, and Social Sciences.

[44] A deciding factor here is what part the fine arts are permitted to play in the curriculum. In places where they have achieved status equal to the other fields, they are often made into a separate division; in colleges where their status is on a non-credit or part-credit basis, they are more usually tied to another field, or else treated as extra-curricular.

[45] *Whitman College Catalogue,* 1942.

sidual outlines of the prescribed curriculum of the nineteenth century, although the actual choice of some of the subjects is left up to the student. A freshman year prescription from one college of this kind, for instance, reads: English, Bible, a foreign language, History, two Sciences, and Physical Education.

In summary, the division- or group-sampling plans do not propose any particular new ideas as to how general education is discovered in the curriculum. Rather, their assumption is that a "good, all-round introduction" to whatever range of subjects their curriculums may offer is, after all, the best definition of "general education" which that college could wish to provide.

Integrated subject-matter plans.

A growing feeling that the division-sampling plan was at best a haphazard way of guaranteeing "acquaintance with the great fields of knowledge" is said by W. W. Charters [46] to have inspired the development of plans which tried to integrate the offerings of a whole subject-matter division into one course, for the consumption of all. This led to that major twentieth century educational phenomenon, the survey course.[47]

The first survey course is commonly agreed to have been Columbia's "Contemporary Civilization," which grew out of a course on War Aims in 1917. For fifteen years after that the growth was slow.[48] In the last eleven years the survey course has mushroomed, so that by the end of 1941, out of 350 colleges asked, 170 reported giving survey courses of some kind, and several others announced close equivalents, in the form of "orientation" courses.

That a survey course is being given is easier for colleges to report than what, by definition, they consider it to be. Charters proposes:

A broad, integrated course cutting across departmental lines, prepared for students who wish to secure a "cultured layman's" under-

[46] "General Survey Courses," *Journal of Higher Education*, Vol. 13, pp. 1–4, January, 1942.
[47] See, e.g., B. Lamar Johnson (edr.), *What About Survey Courses?* 1937.
[48] Charters, *op. cit.*, p. 3. (whole paragraph from his data.)

standing of the nature and contributions of large divisions of knowledge—an end course in general education.[49]

A good deal of confusion will be found, even after acceptance of such a definition as this, over the distinctions if any between "survey" and "orientation" courses. Scroggs'[50] rather courageous attempt to distinguish three types of courses does not, unfortunately, jibe too well with Charters'. According to Scroggs, the orientation course aims to cut across related departments; the survey course aims at a bird's eye view of one large, integrated field; and the "general course"—which Scroggs evidently prefers—"attempts a re-synthesis of knowledge around those general concepts that run through the entire field, with the presentation of sufficient detail to give those general concepts meaning." [51]

Admitting this vagueness in one more area of the general education problem, the operations of the survey course (using this term generically, for convenience) are certainly broad in scope and usually most painstakingly organized. In size they vary widely. A single history course may be served up survey-style, as "a survey of American Art since 1700." Or the survey course may embrace, at the other extreme, the total offering of one great division of knowledge over a period of two years, as in Columbia's "Contemporary Civilization," or in the four introductory courses at the University of Chicago.

The lengthy menu of the survey course, plus the fact that it is usually prescribed for all students within the college or, at least, within one division, necessitates some means of systematic evaluation. Thus a companion innovation of the survey course has become the comprehensive examination. This has reached perhaps its most highly developed form at Chicago, where it functions as the sole means of deciding the student's fitness to pass on to the Senior College (junior year).

Why has the survey course grown so fast and so widely on the college scene? First, it is an economical device, since it centers

[49] *Ibid.*, p. 2.
[50] Scroggs, *op. cit.*, pp. 147–148.
[51] *Ibid.*, p. 148.

students, staff, and materials in one main course of activity. Second, it is administratively efficient, for this same centralizing reason. Third, it is felt to provide for all students in the college a democratizing, collectivizing study experience, a thing held important in these times. As the authors of the book *The Chicago College Plan* say:

These five examinations (at the end of the four introductory courses, plus an English qualifying test) represent a common core of educational experience and background for all students who complete the requirements of our College: they constitute the major part of our definition of general education.[52]

The survey-course technique thus sees general education as a problem involving the need for a more vital presentation of the same great areas of subject matter viewed by the division-sampling plans. At the same time, a curious requisite of this newer trend is that, almost willy-nilly, it is returning the college program for the first two years to a seventy-five-to-one-hundred per cent prescribed system, a situation which has not been the case since the end of the past century. Perhaps within this "New Prescription" a wide enough freedom can obtain (witness the no-credit-hours, no-regular-attendance system at Chicago) more than to compensate for the loss of student's subject-choosing option. Still—although the chief purpose of this chapter is expository rather than critical—there seems some reason to review, in conclusion, a warning made ten years ago by George A. Works, then Dean of Students at Chicago:

In recent years there has been a pronounced movement toward a differentiation between the lower and the upper two years of the college curriculum. This movement has been accompanied by a distinct tendency toward a larger measure of prescription . . . than has previously obtained. . . . It is also represented in recent years in the very general development of orientation courses, and of introductory and general courses of various kinds. It should be recognized that in a measure, at least, this is a movement opposite in character from those movements previously considered, since it has as its purpose the requirement of a common experience on the part of all students. *In general they do not represent adaptation to in-*

[52] C. S. Boucher and A. J. Brumbaugh, p. 20. 1940.

dividuals, but call for adaptation on the part of individuals to a common body of experience.[53]

A second type of integrated subject-matter plan, entirely different from the survey-course idea, can hardly be called a "trend," since it is being tried out just now in only one college. Yet its advent and argument in the past five years have stirred up such an academic uproar that it must be included in this survey. This, of course, is the Hutchins-St. John's Great Books plan. The plan, as few now need be told, involves a four-year course built upon the digestion (with extensive laboratory work when relevant) of one hundred classic books, ranging from ancient Greece to the Western World of the late nineteenth century (Bertrand Russell is the only contemporary on the list).

A program centered about a list of discrete books could hardly be called "integrated" in the quantitative sense of the survey course. Rather than this, the integration is deemed to lie in the integrative value of each and all of these great books toward the gaining of a truly "liberal" education. As the catalog states, "They are the real teachers." [54]

We have here, therefore, a plan geared to meet the demands stated by Hutchins in *The Higher Learning in America*:

> We have then for general education a course of study consisting of the greatest books of the western world and the arts of reading, writing, thinking (grammar, rhetoric, and logic) and speaking, together with mathematics, the best exemplar of the processes of human reason.[55]

As such, this plan for the purpose of general education seems formally to accept only a part of one of the above-mentioned four groups of aims for general education (see page 35), namely, the qualitative growth of the individual (mind). There is no place made, at least in the specific course of study, for contemporary fact about the world and society, or for direct

---

[53] In W. S. Gray (edr.), *Provision for the Individual in College Education*, p. 77. 1932. Italics mine.
[54] *St. John's College, Catalogue for 1941-42*, p. 17.
[55] R. M. Hutchins, p. 85. 1936.

motivation, on the strength of the study-course alone, toward larger service in the society of today. Whether St. John's' achievement of its one centered aim will be so brilliant that it manages to fill the gaps left by the rest; whether, in other words, the St. John's graduate, with his brand of liberal education, will himself more than make up for this absence of contemporary reference in his formal college learning; or whether (as is argued by the plan's supporters) the actual methods of the college—its teaching, activities, and over-all life—more than make up any such formal deficiencies;—these are questions to which a large number of curious ears on the college scene during the next few years will listen for hints of an answer.

Functional-needs plans.

Temperamentally as far as the moon from the plan just mentioned are those colleges which have built their programs for general education squarely upon what they see to be the immediate and future needs of modern youth. In a sense these programs, too, must be called "integrated subject-matter" plans, since their eventual form is typically a series of survey or orientation courses, which are taken by all. Their content, however, is largely different, and stems from entirely different roots.

The motivation for programs of this kind was supplied in the 1930's by several studies of youth problems arising from the depression.[56] The conclusions of these studies agreed that to a large proportion of college youth, economic security is the big problem, followed by a need for social and creative opportunities denied them by an urbanized, industrialized modern life. General education, according to interpreters of these views, should aim directly at these and other areas of direct need.[57]

The most ambitious acceptance of such a challenge has been at the General College of Minnesota. After a large-scale two-year program of research in the achievements, capacities, needs,

[56] See, e.g., H. P. Rainey, *How Fare American Youth*, a Report to the American Youth Commission of the American Council on Education. 1938.

[57] N.S.S.E., *General Education in the American College*. See chapter by Rainey, "Social Factors Affecting General Education," pp. 15–27.

interests, and attitudes of its students and former students, the
staff of the General College in 1938 worked out a curriculum
of four main "orientation areas": [58] Individual Orientation;
Home Life Orientation; Socio-Civic Orientation; and Vocational Orientation. (Additional areas are offered, in Biological
Sciences; Euthenics; General Arts; Human Development; Literature, Speech, and Writing; and Physical Sciences. The
orientation courses are urged for all, though officially not required.) Evaluation is by means of comprehensive examination, checked continually by a technically-equipped Committee on Educational Research.

A similar type of plan, somewhat less concrete, forms the
core of the curriculum at Stephens Junior College for women.
Here, under the leadership of W. W. Charters, research into
the over-all needs of contemporary young women led to the
construction of a program of courses in seven major areas: [59]
communication; aesthetics; physical health; mental health;
consumer's problems; social relations; and philosophy of living.

The functional-needs plans thus take a fairly literal stand
upon the question of what should go into a general education.
Seizing the facts and ideas which are found to be wrapped up
in the life of a young American in these times, they build a
program in which those facts and principles are directly dealt
with as both subject *and reference* of the course of study. They
base claims for authority upon the fact that their curriculum
is the result of asking their students "what they really need in
general education." [60] The program must therefore be judged
upon the validity of this method.

In terms of this chapter's discussion, however, another question needs to be asked. Can the "qualitative" type of individual growth—that is, growth in his precision, his appreciation,
his working attitudes and ideals, etc.—be handled by this kind
of direct, one-to-one quantitative approach? Can the begin-

[58] See Bulletin of the University of Minnesota, *General College of the University, 1940–41.*

[59] B. Lamar Johnson, "General Education Changes the College," *Bulletin of
the Association of American Colleges,* Vol. 24, pp. 229–234, May, 1938.

[60] Bulletin of the University of Minnesota, *op. cit.,* p. 23.

nings of a "philosophy of life," for instance, be "taught" to each student via the classroom, by incorporating it in one section of an orientation course? Questions like these, it can be hoped, will become more and more the business of the evaluation committee, in the future of general education programs of this kind.

Work-plans.

To talk here about work-plans for general education in a way breaks the rule set at the outset, namely, that the discussion should involve only changes in the actual curriculum. On the other hand, work-activities on some campuses have actually come to an estate where they must with justice be called part of the teaching program. This, however, is not true at all colleges which advertise work-programs. In fact, most of these still suffer from the inability to see work-experience as quite "nice," from a liberally educative point of view. This discussion concerns, therefore, only that type of plan which has actually tried to integrate work and classroom study together. Examples are still few.

The integration of campus and outside work into the regular activities of the program, moreover, may proceed from a variety of motives, which grade from the opportune to the educational. The distinction in many cases is difficult to make. Enough to say, colleges with the former emphasis use student work on campus and elsewhere primarily to reduce costs to students or college for the maintenance of the program, or else to prepare the student for an occupation, stressing meanwhile that such work is adding to the student's "general" education. Colleges emphasizing the educational side of work, on the other hand, tend to prescribe it regardless of direct financial need or lack of need. More than that, they try actually to incorporate the facts and values of the work-experiences into the student's classroom learning. Owing partly perhaps to the unavoidable *ad hoc* demands and rewards of the workaday world, almost all colleges have found this harder than it sounds.

A plan which has tried to move in the direction of extract-

ing the educative value from work during the school year is
the so-called Cooperative System. Although it is thought first
to have started at the College of Engineering of the University
of Cincinnati in 1906,[61] the best-known example in the liberal
college field is Antioch. There the familiar pattern is to alter-
nate ten (sometimes five) weeks in college with the same in
gainful employment away, each schedule being shared by two
students, working the shift. When possible, the work chosen
is that which will tie in somehow with the student's educational interests. The cooperative work-plan operates along
with a normal regimen of academic fields, subjects, and courses
at the college.[62]

In addition to their function to show the importance of work
in a modern general education, college work-plans as a part of
the educational program thus try, at least by inference, to rea-
lize Deweyan concepts of learning by doing. The present difficulty in this seems to involve how to make the "doing" and the
"learning" center more closely upon the same thing. The integration of work-learning with study-learning is easier in the
technical schools, where student careers can already be identified in a general occupational reference.[63] In the liberal arts
education such a task becomes admittedly hard. At Antioch,
for instance, the claim is stated merely,[64] "The cooperative plan
. . . is a vital part of a liberal arts program, and is *supplementary* to the academic program."

For the purpose of an integrated general education, then,
efforts toward a closer marriage of the values from work with
those from study, in the liberal arts college, may in the future
be expected to capitalize the progress made so far, and then
move somewhere farther along.

[61] University of Cincinnati Bulletin, *Cooperative Courses, College of Engineering and Commerce, 1942–1943,* p. 14.

[62] Another interesting feature at Antioch, though outside the province of this
discussion, is their Community Government, organized to implement large-scale
student-initiative in running the business and life of the college campus—surely
a large potential catalyst to the academic program of general education.

[63] See, e.g., the Bulletin of the Rochester Athenaeum and Mechanics Institute,
Individualized Education. December, 1937.

[64] Antioch College Bulletin, *Catalog Issue, 1941–1942.* Italics mine.

Semi-individualized plans.

The four (or really, five) types of plans so far mentioned have agreed in one important way: they all believe that, whatever the program eventually decided upon, its content should be made common to all. Agreement on this point is not universal in the American college. In certain notable centers, the belief is rather that dedicating educational aims to the individual's development is rather meaningless if it neglects the rock-bottom fact of individual differences. To these colleges, a curricular program common to all (no matter what individualized procedures may be used to put it across) does do some essential damage to that "rock-bottom fact." This type of view is interpreted by Capen:

. . . The end of college education is the cultivation of certain abilities and attitudes of mind, not the acquisition of a special body of information, and . . . the imposition of any general prescription is likely to interfere with the cultivation of these abilities and attitudes.[65]

The first two-year program in colleges which accept this view tend to take on varying degrees of departure from the prescribed-content system. For convenience they are schematized here as "semi" and "largely" individualized programs.

The "semi" type, the concern of this section, proceeds upon a divisional organization of subject-fields, and allows the student to take all or most of his work within a single division of his choice. Concentration within a division starts one or two years after entrance;[66] but the courses taken previous to entrance into the division are usually picked to help prepare for the particular divisional work to follow.

This system, it can be seen, thus permits a sort of specialization usually possible only in graduate school, and subject only

[65] University of Buffalo Bulletin, *Reports of the Chancellor and the Comptroller*, p. 16. November, 1935.

[66] Olivet College Bulletin, *General Information*, Vol. 39, April, 1940; and University of Buffalo Bulletin, *The College of Arts and Sciences*, Vol. 30, February, 1942.

to whatever administrative checks may be felt wise.[67] General education therefore, according to this system, must be seen almost wholly in a non-quantitative light. The requirements that each student come, through formal course work, at least to meet the "major facts about his world" are not accepted. Seen against the plans described above (except possibly the St. John's plan), this represents a fairly major break in educational thought, which must expect to receive a good deal of outside challenge.

At the same time, this type of program, as advanced for instance by Buffalo University and Olivet College, must face a challenge on another front, which is their own chosen one. How far does their individualization really go? Despite the divisional specializing allowed, the core of the program is still *a system of courses.* What follows, then, can only in part, after all, be geared to the student's individual mind and needs.

This type of plan, in other words, diagnoses the educational problem differently for each separate student; still, it treats that problem by means of a pattern of courses which are, by and large, as conventional as those at any college. The *choice,* not the actual *composition,* of the subject-field to be studied is the nub, then, of this kind of individuation.[68] It does not, probably for sound and practical reasons, choose to travel farther along the road.

Largely individualized-program plans: the progressive college programs.

In 1932 Kathryn McHale, prefacing her edited list of expert contemporary opinions on the future of liberal arts education, passed an interesting set of predictions:

One could only hazard a guess as to what exactly will constitute the curriculum ten years hence or in what way learning will be guided. It may be safe, however, to assert as general characteristics of the future that the curriculum will integrate fields of learning;

[67] See *ibid.,* p. 34, "To guard against undue specialization . . . students will be required to take 72 semester hours outside their field of concentration."

[68] From here on, this word will be used instead of the longer, clumsier "individualization."

that both curriculum and method will be individualized, and differ-
entiated in terms of individual capacity, interest, and future needs;
that teaching will be more exact but more informal; and that the
student will be socialized through contacts with many more life
situations and will be able to learn more completely by living more
completely.[69]

The attempt to fill at least one of these predictions—"that
both curriculum and method will be individualized"—is a fair
introduction to the progressive college programs as worked out
at Sarah Lawrence, Bennington, and Bard Colleges. Since
these colleges are the basis for the rest of this study, no attempt
should be made here to describe them even in summary manner. To round out the description of plans of general education in the American college today, however, the point at which
their operations, particularly in the first two years, depart from
the other types may be briefly noted.

Like the semi-individualized plans just described, the progressive college programs require no official introduction to
over-all bodies of fact or ideas. They stress the qualitative and
unique nature of individual growth. The implications in this,
they believe, call for a tailor-made curriculum and large-scale
student responsibility. This, however, they have interpreted
more literally than have the other colleges. Not only is the
student's program allowed at college entrance to concentrate in
chosen areas (with, again, various formal and informal administrative checks), but, in large degree, *the core of what the individual student studies is not "courses," but whatever he and
his adviser construct it to be.* It is, therefore, in part at least, a
system of tutorials, in which the tutorials become, not aids to
course-work, but substitutes for the courses themselves, over a
four-year period.

This tutorial "core," it should be added, is surrounded by
group, class, laboratory, and field work, much of which takes
form as more or less conventional "courses." Regulation and
evaluation are done largely by the adviser and various faculty
committees constituted for this purpose. "Grades," in the con-

[69] N.S.S.E., *Changes and Experiments in Liberal Arts Education,* p. 235.

ventional sense, do not exist. Examinations are given only when in the individual case it appears useful.[70]

As a last point relevant to general education, less distinction than usual is made between "curricular" and "extra-curricular" on these campuses, since the former is construed broadly enough to take in most of the latter.

Such, in barest essence, are the points of departure in the progressive college programs. The rest of this study attempts to fill out and explain this picture: first, by giving available details of certain parts of the college structures, from their beginnings to the present time; second, by a report of personal discussion with fifty members of the three staffs on the ideas behind these programs; and last, by reviewing the collected evidence to consider what "general education" comes to mean when seen in the frame of reference which the progressive colleges have provided.

SUMMARY

To summarize the problems in this chapter, and at the same time to indicate the ground which the following chapters hope to cover, four questions may be posed. The present position of these issues, as has been demonstrated in the foregoing discussion, makes their statement as questions the only justifiable form:

1. What is the case for prescribing a coverage of certain large content-areas, as a method in general education?

2. What does "individual growth through education" mean, in terms of the methods the college can use to deal with it?

3. How can a college program be truly effective in promoting "social education," in the small and large sense?

4. After these questions have been considered, where do the progressive college programs stand, as actual or potential contributors to the improvement of aims and methods in general education in the American college?

[70] Meanwhile, it should be reported at once that Bennington (starting the fall of 1942) has launched a new program in which the tutorial core is retained but substantially changed, and the course-work greatly enhanced, especially in the direction of integrated subject matter. The issues underlying these changes will figure prominently in later discussion.

Chapter III

The Sarah Lawrence Program

GENERAL INTRODUCTION

THE systematic study of a college's program, as mentioned in Chapter II, has typically taken one of two forms, the external and the internal.[1] The former type usually is made up of a committee of outside experts on college education, who have been subsidized for the purpose. The internal type (which is becoming the more common) is made by the college itself, through the work of part or all of its own staff. Both types of studies habitually take months and even years. If possible, they use every kind of evaluative device helpful to the problem, to get at length a body of results which can be used there and elsewhere as a more or less official statement of what the college in question "adds up to" at the time.

In the case of this study, made by a student of college education unattached to any of the three colleges in view, an extended survey of the kinds mentioned was not possible. The aim, moreover, (providentally, perhaps) was of a different sort. It was not to try to find what three colleges "add up to," in terms of some computable results. Rather it was (1) to review, at each college, the significant choices and changes in the educational program from founding to present; (2) in some degree, to crystallize the major trends of thinking that have moved behind these choices and changes. To the extent that much of educational thinking becomes clear only in the actual "choices and changes" that result from it, separation of parts (1) and (2) of the aim is not feasible. In the main, however, it may be said the emphasis of Chapters III to VI will be on facts about the progressive college programs, while the emphasis of Chapter

[1] See Eells, *Surveys of American Higher Education.* 1937.

49

VII will be on the ideas in which these facts seem to find their source.

Again, it should be made clear that to give a "thumb-nail history" of each of the three colleges is not the intent. The assignment has been taken on, to interpret the progressive college programs in the light of "general education." With this regard, the discussion of the college programs considers four topics: (1) primary college aims; (2) the course and method of study; (3) evaluation and control; (4) admissions policies. The approach is from the over-all administrative side and thus necessarily avoids specific mention of problems within subject-fields. Lastly, the analysis is submitted as covering only those high spots of the programs which become visible to the outside student through a year and a half's reading, conversing, and observing in connection with the three colleges in view.

SARAH LAWRENCE

The original picture.

Sarah Lawrence was provisionally chartered as a two-year Junior College [2] in December, 1926, the first higher institution with less than a four-year program to be granted a charter by the Regents of the University of the State of New York.[3] Its founding was the result of William V. Lawrence's benefaction of $1,250,000; a half-million of this was represented by his Bronxville mansion and grounds which became the college campus. (From this money, three dormitories, and other college buildings, were built before college opening.) Mr. Lawrence, then eighty-three, formed a board of trustees with the help of President H. N. MacCracken of Vassar College, who served as the first Chairman. Miss Marion Coats, who had initiated an experimental plan at Bradford Junior College, was chosen president; and during the two years until the college opened (October, 1928), she worked out the program upon the

[2] Much of the ensuing data comes from Miss Constance Warren's "President's Report on the First Ten Years of Sarah Lawrence College" (mimeographed), 1936.

[3] M. Coats, "A New Type of Junior College," *Journal of the National Education Association*, Vol. 18, pp. 5–6, January, 1929.

general plan for "a new type of women's college" [4] which Mr. Lawrence with the help of Dr. MacCracken had proposed. A statement of this program was issued, along with an invitation for faculty applications; the tentative staff assembled in December, 1927; and the college opened, ten months later, with a total of 216 students, of which 156 lived in the college. Since that time the enrollment has been purposely held to somewhat less than three hundred, most of the growth having been made possible by the building of a fourth dormitory, in 1931.

A major outside change was consummated in 1931, when the college obtained a permanent charter as a four-year institution with power to give the B.A. degree. The single change in administration to date was in 1929; Miss Constance Warren, formerly Head of Pine Manor Junior College, became President.

Primary college aims. [5]

From the first it has been clear that the founders and heads of Sarah Lawrence wished it to be a new departure in women's education. Mr. Lawrence himself, according to President Warren, [6] wanted a college to "provide for girls of good minds a women's education, not a man's, which would:

(1) stimulate intellectual interests to be self-perpetuating
(2) appreciate leisure and use it constructively
(3) obtain group experience which would show the value of cooperative effort, train through this both leaders and followers.
(4) provide special opportunities for the gifted."

These aims, except the last one, were used by President Coats almost without change in the first college catalog: (1927–28)

"1. To graduate women in whom intellectual interest has been so stimulated that it will continue as an animating principle throughout life.
2. To graduate women whose experience in group activities has shown them the value of cooperative effort, so that either they

[4] *Sarah Lawrence College Catalog, 1927–28*, p. 45.
[5] This is a discussion of over-all, directional aims. Working aims, e.g., those bearing on method and clientele, are discussed in later sections.
[6] Warren, *op. cit.*, p. 19.

become fruitful as leaders, or skilled in rendering intelligent support to the effective leadership of others.

3. To graduate women who have experienced the value of leisure and whose varied interests insure the profitable use of whatever leisure time shall be theirs." [7]

Part of the desire for a departure from conventional higher education was involved in the administrative fact of a two-year college. Such a unit, President Coats believed, was more in keeping with the type of education for the young women that Mr. Lawrence, and she herself, had in mind. This idea carried with it a dissatisfaction with the ultra-academic brand of learning of most contemporary women's colleges, especially when applied to girls not intending to stay four years (see section on admissions, below). A first important underlying aim, in other words, became the desire for a different kind of scholarship, one which, though "strictly collegiate in character" [8] (the college must not be thought another preparatory or finishing school), would avoid the rarefied atmosphere of the college dominated by graduate-school academic thinking. Positively put, this was stated,[9] "The first two years of college are valuable primarily for the information yielded by the experience of living." (It is interesting to note here how closely Miss Coats' idea parallels that held by many today [see Chap. II] as to what should be one of the chief aims for a program of general education.)

With the foregoing area of objectives thus staked out it seems at first a paradox that Sarah Lawrence should have turned into a four-year college, granting the B.A. degree. The answer has been given by the college, however, that this did not mean a turnover to the type of learning commonly associated with the four-year, B.A. college course; rather it meant Sarah Lawrence considered her program essentially good enough to stand for the

[7] *Sarah Lawrence College Catalog, 1927–28*, p. 17.

[8] Coats, *op. cit.*, p. 5.

[9] *Ibid.* cf. also *Sarah Lawrence College Catalog, 1927–28*, "Statement by Dr. Henry Noble MacCracken," p. 7: ". . . it will differ from the four-year college in that it will provide a cultural training only and that the method used will be that of training rather than research."

baccalaureate degree on a par with the other liberal colleges. The New York Regents' grant of charter in 1931 officially sanctioned this claim.[10]

Facts behind the situation show that the change was not so much a revolution in objectives as a development from them. Although Miss Coats stressed the experimental convenience of the two-year college unit, the provisional charter allowed the college to offer, if it chose, two, three, or four years of work. Anticipating the change, perhaps, Miss Warren wrote in 1930, "It opened as a two-year college of liberal arts, but whether it stops at two years or develops three or four years of work is incidental."[11]

As to the downright quality of teaching and learning, measured by conventional liberal arts college standards, the intention from the first was that it should be "equal to the best colleges for women so far as concerns the standard of scholarship, the method of instruction, and the satisfaction by examination (though this method has changed) of the completion of courses."[12] Although the clientele was to be of a somewhat special sort (see section on admissions, below), its quality likewise was to be held high. There is no evidence anywhere in other words, of an idea that this should be in the least degree a kind of "bonehead" college.

The decision as to whether the Sarah Lawrence program was suitable to become a four-year course toward the B.A. degree, therefore, must rest not upon the issue of two versus four years, but upon one's philosophy of what liberal arts education should be in the present day. If Miss Coats's original ideas for Sarah Lawrence are logically expanded to apply to the four-year program, the philosophy becomes, a course of study which (1) avoids the graduate-research type of learning and (2) stresses instead learning which has to do with "the experience of liv-

[10] The two-year diploma, meanwhile, is still given to those who wish to complete only half the course.
[11] C. Warren, "The Sarah Lawrence Plan," *Nation*, Vol. 131, pp. 549–550, November 19, 1930.
[12] *Sarah Lawrence College Catalog, 1927–28*, "Statement by Dr. H. N. MacCracken," p. 7.

ing." [13] On the strength of this position, then, the aim of the Sarah Lawrence program toward the bachelor's degree in liberal arts must be judged. [14]

If the nature of the Sarah Lawrence program from the first has had to do primarily with "the information gained from the experience of living," it can be as readily shown that the chief focus for that program has been *the individual student and her needs*. This is so basically true that it is literally impossible to read a statement of the college's aims without noting that they uniformly are made to revolve about the individual girl. Three quotations from, respectively, early, middle-period, and recent statements about the college may illustrate the unwaveringness of this gospel:

These new colleges should study carefully the peculiar aptitudes and interests of students as they graduate from high school, and should rebuild college programs to conform to the facts disclosed by such studies. [15] (1927)

From the start the aim and effort have been to plan the work for the individual student. [16] (1933)

It follows that the college is experimental in nature. It must find more effective ways of recognizing the differences between one student and another in capacity, needs, interests, ways of working; of selecting appropriate materials and methods for each student; and of helping each student to assume increasing responsibility for significant self-direction. [17] (1941)

Such dedications to the individual and his needs, it may be recalled from Chapter I, are not uncommon among college-catalog statements in general. It remains to be seen below what kind of methods were worked out in this case to try to match

[13] That this *is* still the philosophy of the program is borne out in the statement of the current catalog (1941–42), p. 8: "Thus the aim is that education shall always consist of meaningful experiences."

[14] Such a "judgment"—though it is hardly escapable in the undercurrents of the whole study—is not the direct concern of this chapter.

[15] *Sarah Lawrence College Catalog, 1927–28*, "Statement by Miss Marion Coats," p. 13.

[16] B. Doershuck, "Statement," *Bulletin of the Association of American Colleges*, Vol. 19, p. 111, March, 1933.

[17] *Sarah Lawrence College Catalog, 1941–42*, "Foreword," p. 5.

the stated individual-centered aims. First, however, a final area of "primary aims" should be reviewed.

In the preceding chapter it was brought out that most contemporary programs for general education have two foci of attention for their aims, the individual and, more recently, society. In the frame of that reference, the first focus, at Sarah Lawrence, has been shown to be almost uniquely important. What about the other?

Above also it was argued that the society-centered focus for educational aims has gained most of its sharpness since the early depression years of the past decade. If this is true, strong aims of the social kind might hardly be expected in a college program of 1927, the year that the Sarah Lawrence plan was formed; the appeal to the individual, on the other hand, would typically have the major sway. A reading of the college catalog for this first year, plus the formal announcement of the program by Miss Coats, also in 1927,[18] shows this to be very much the case (see her list of primary aims, above, p. 51). One notes, for instance, that although "group activities" are an important part of the program, the gain from these activities is to be primarily the individual's, not the group's. There seems, in fact, some superficial resemblance of the proverbial ivory tower, to the extent that the early college affirmed Mr. Lawrence's wish that "beauty" be its theme, and the first president stated, "It is the desire of the college to surround the student with beautiful equipment." [19]

Unlike the steadfast individual-centered aims, however, this last situation, showing in an interesting way the hand of a changing outside society, has itself shown a change. A review of Sarah Lawrence statements since 1930 reveals a decided upgrading in references to the girl's need to be prepared for life and work in contemporary society. At first the reference is apt to appear more or less as an afterthought. In the 1930–31 catalog, one reads:

[18] M. Coats, "Sarah Lawrence College Statutes of Instruction" (mimeographed), 1927.

[19] M. Coats, "A New Type of Junior College," *Journal of the N.E.A.*, Vol. 18, p. 6.

The liberal arts, today, are those studies that lead to broader generalization of natural law, to wider application of this knowledge, to higher reaches of the imaginative impulse, *to a more generous attitude* toward society.[20]

Two years later, somewhat more concrete social objectives can be seen:

By regarding the student as a member of an intelligent, cooperating group made up of all students and faculty, the college tries to help her fit herself for the responsibilities and privileges of mature living.[21]

Here it can be noticed that the "group" referred to is used in a restricted sense, i.e., the immediate, campus group. A year later, however, this is seen in a reference to that society reaching beyond campus walls:

A college situation of this sort, with students of varied background, and faculty who are participating actively in home and civic life, is no ivory tower where a student may retreat from "real life." It is rather a sector of real life where a student may secure the most adequate preparation for subsequent participation in and adjustment to a changing world.[22]

In the catalog for 1936–37, in the section "College Organization," a definite social aim is found. This statement rests unchanged in the current (1941–42) catalog. It may be noted, though, that the characteristic individual approach is kept:

The common aim is the development of social responsibility; a synthesis of work, recreation, social life; a sense of comparative values in the use of time. *Freedom of choice is essential for the development of such responsibility.*[23]

If the sense of this last sounds still too much restricted to the local scene, President Warren's opening two sentences in chapter nine, "Education for Social Responsibility," of her recent book on the work of Sarah Lawrence, lend evidence of an affirmation by the college of contemporary social aims, along with its individual ones:

[20] *Sarah Lawrence College Catalog, 1930–31*, p. 10.
[21] *Sarah Lawrence College Catalog, 1932–33*, p. 15.
[22] *Ibid., 1934–35*, p. 9.
[23] *Ibid., 1936–37*, p. 52. Italics mine.

Colleges must be concerned today with educating young people for social responsibility. By which I mean educating them not only to an awareness of community responsibility but also to be active participants in the maintenance of democracy itself.[24]

Thus, the aims of Sarah Lawrence at the present time are shown to be dedicated to (1) the medium of the liberal arts, geared not so much to the traditional academic approach as to the contemporary experience of living; (2) the individual as *end and method* of the educative process; (3) the individual's active adjustment to society, an aim which is to be approached, at the same time, through *the individual's own particular point of reference*.

What that method, involving so much the individual, has been worked out to be during the college's educational history should next be studied. Otherwise, sincere though they be, the aims just stated like so many that have been read may be allowed to sink out of sight in the general morass of college-aims vocabulary.

The course and method of study.

The original aims for the Sarah Lawrence program have been stated to be concerned with "living" education and "individual" education. To implement the first, "curriculum" was at the start made to take in three areas: academic subjects, "group activities," and "leisure time." The latter two will be discussed in the latter part of this section.[25]

Methods of individual study. Concerning the early study-subjects in the college, the first thing to be noted is that in identity and content they were actually quite like those in conventional colleges. The method of selection, furthermore, was the traditional group-sampling plan. To qualify for graduation (two years) a girl must have completed six courses, selected from the following groups: "Arts" (including English); foreign languages (French, German, Greek, and Latin); natural sciences; and social sciences.

[24] C. Warren, *A New Design for Women's Education*, p. 181. 1940.

[25] Data on the early program from *Sarah Lawrence College Catalog, 1927–28*, and "Sarah Lawrence College Statutes of Instruction" by Miss Coats (1927).

A first discovery, then, is that *what* was studied, so far as courses are concerned, was not in itself individualized or vitalized in the original program. Rather, the "vital" element was to be the teacher's creative way of handling the traditional subject matter. About this, for instance, President Coats proposed:

The content of the curriculum recognizes the value of "significant situations" in motivating the academic work of the students. Instead of teaching theories which may or may not be found to apply to the concrete cases met in later life, the fellows (teachers) invite the students to make inductive studies of their own, using any serious materials found in daily life.[26]

As for the individualizing, this, in those first days, apparently was to be the function not so much of the content as of the method of study. Each course had a syllabus; these syllabi were divided into four- or six-weeks units of assignments which the student then set out, much on her own, to fulfill. The time for the fulfillment of these study-contracts could be adjusted to suit the individual case. The instructor was available in his office each morning for consultation; in addition, he usually held during the week two hours of more or less formal class.

It is true that a tutorial base such as this could hardly help resulting in a fair degree of individuation of the actual content of what was studied. This, too, was officially sanctioned:

The academic work of a single "course" must pass readily across conventional subject boundary lines as the interests and needs of the individual students dictate.[27]

In the main, however, the content of the course, in the first year of the Sarah Lawrence program, appears to have lagged behind the method used in the matter of suiting itself to the individual need. This remained essentially true in the early period of President Warren's administration. The catalog for 1930–31 states the position at that time:

[26] M. Coats, "A New Type of Junior College," p. 5.
[27] Coats, "Sarah Lawrence College Statutes of Instruction," p. 18.

The curriculum of Sarah Lawrence College consists, therefore, of the recognized formal disciplines of our time. *The experimental element enters in trying out new approaches, fresh materials, untested methods* for these departments of study.[28]

These methods Miss Warren listed elsewhere [29] at that time as, primarily: small number of courses; large degree of independent work; small classes, individual conferences, and the don system; "activities" intra- not extra-curriculum; continued field work, including much use of New York City, and of neighboring communities; qualitative evaluation of the student; and a faculty sold on an experimental attitude toward teaching. Almost without exception, the same basic methods stand unchanged today.

In line with the study's underlying topic of general education, it is interesting finally to note that the girls were expected, sometime in their two years, to take work in each of the four fields. Although the early catalogs broadened the requirement with the initial statement that there were no required courses at Sarah Lawrence, the four-field program was specifically mentioned as "the usual thing" until the catalog for 1935–36. In this year there occurred a curriculum-change which must be reviewed below.

Thus the vitality and individuality of course-subjects in the early years of the college seem to have rested less in the content of the courses than in the hands of those whose job it was to put it across. Regarding this last, the keystone of the program, as Miss Coats said in her Statutes, was (and still is) the "don." For each of his five to ten "donnees," the don (adviser) was given much responsibility. Since the Sarah Lawrence girl takes but three courses, his share of her actual instruction was bound to be large. According to the original plan, moreover, he was to "help her select a motivating principle . . . for the year, and to correlate all her activities with reference to that principle." [30] Even more, the don was "urged to help the student

---

[28] *Sarah Lawrence College Catalog, 1930–31*, p. 12. Italics mine.
[29] C. Warren, "The Sarah Lawrence Plan," *Nation*, Vol. 131, p. 549–550, 1930.
[30] Coats, *op. cit.*, p. 11.

form right attitudes toward life," [31] all in all, a rather large prescription for one poor pedagog.

Whatever his success with assignments like the last, in 1931 the don's work was facilitated in one sense and surely made harder in another by the abolition of the syllabus plan. As the Director of Education (an office similar to academic dean), Miss Beatrice Doershuck, commented, "A syllabus prepared in advance was bound to be quite incompatible with adjustment of work to individual needs for training and for the development of interests." [32] In its place, the deciding of *what* the girl was to study, as well as its correlation, began to become a matter up to the don and his advisee. And so the individuation of content as well as method in this college's program was allowed to proceed considerably further upon its way.

In 1935, receipt of a grant from the General Education Board for the purpose of experimenting in teaching problems, including specifically the problem of orienting the entering student to college work,[33] gave rise to the freshman exploratory course, a device which now is a prime feature of the Sarah Lawrence program. The exploratory courses, as described in a recent study, are "planned with the intention of following through for every freshman whatever educational leads the teacher is able to get, for the principal purpose of helping to direct the student's further education." [34] In substance, the exploratory course bases itself in various areas and problems within a large subject-field. As such, its outside appearance has led some onlookers to call it simply another kind of survey course. This impression the teachers of the exploratory courses go to some lengths to correct. The fundamental difference, it is pointed out, is that the exploratory course aims at centering itself not in some organization of subject matter but in *the ideas of the students*. Once the topic is set for the course, the

---

[31] *Ibid.*, p. 12.

[32] Doershuck, *op. cit.*, p. 111.

[33] The three books reporting the results of this study are R. Munroe, *Teaching the Individual;* L. B. Murphy, *Psychology for Individual Education;* E. Raushenbush, *Literature for Individual Education.*

[34] Raushenbush, *op. cit.*, p. 22.

work and discussion proceeds pretty much as the students and teacher will it. "In the literature course (for instance) books are selected not in terms of a literary type or a literary period, but for the light they throw upon the questions the group has undertaken to discuss." [35]

The exploratory course, in other words, has been developed as an aid, both to the girl and to her teacher, in the efforts to find for her the kind of work she is best able to do as a college student. Since as a rule the freshman has as don the person who teaches the exploratory course she has selected, the exploratory course, as a method, serves as an important extension of the don's activity. On the basis of what the exploratory course has stirred up in the student, much of the individual conference-work with the don can then proceed. Seen thus, it becomes another step toward the individualizing of the content, as well as the method, of the student's education.

A limitation in the exploratory-course technique is that to date no such course has been fully developed in the fields of natural science and fine arts. Instead, these fields (along with the others) list "introductory courses," which approach learning from a viewpoint somewhat closer to the existing organization of the subject matter to be studied. Here again, however, the intent is not primarily a coverage of categorical fact. As a statement about the introductory courses says:

These are not survey courses. They open up general areas of knowledge and experience so that the student may recognize more clearly some field of study or some aspect of the contemporary world. They seek to outline significant problems and acquaint the student with various methods of dealing with them.[36, 37]

At the upperclass level, as might be expected, the orientation of the courses at present is seen even more in terms of the sub-

---

[35] *Ibid.*

[36] *Sarah Lawrence College*, "Outline of Courses for 1941–1942," September 15, 1941 (mimeographed).

[37] The introductory course, at Sarah Lawrence, seems to agree closely, in aim at least, with Scroggs' definition of a "General" course, as given above, Chapter II, p. 38.

ject-field. The assumption might be that students at this level, having found through exploratory and introductory work what they can and like to study, are ready to apply themselves fairly systematically in those directions. What they learn, however, is still kept much in their own reference, through the large degree of individual project and conference work which pervades the teaching methodology of the college as a whole.[38]

To crystallize the foregoing facts about the instructional method in the light of the aims previously discussed, it has been found that the individualizing of the Sarah Lawrence student's program is engineered largely by a semi-formal system of tutorials. The general use of this system, over a period of years, has led by degrees to the individualizing of the actual content of what each student studies. At present, although "courses," with titles, teachers, and classrooms, do exist here as at all colleges, the methods of running the classes are such that what each student pursues *within* these courses now becomes, to a large if varying degree, defined by herself and her teacher as the year goes on. A major intent in the process is that the girl shall gradually find out what she chiefly wants to and can study. The exploratory and introductory courses which she takes during the first two years are geared to this purpose.

In line with the methods of individualizing the learning, finally, no "major" is required. The question of "special study vs. general study," like the question of study-content, is left to be suited to the individual case. (Here is a point of difference from Bard and Bennington, which must be noted further on.) Three types of four-year programs, as a result, are found to be common at Sarah Lawrence: the "cone-type"—i.e., starting with a base of several studies, and gradually proceeding to concentrate on one—; the "inverted cone"—starting at a point of special interest, and then spreading out—; and the "cylinder"— maintaining study, simultaneously throughout the four years, in several different subjects with frequent interconnections. Of these the first type is most common—a fact which may reflect its

---

[38] Individual conferences, at intervals of not more than two weeks, are used in almost all of the college's courses.

logic, or which may on the other hand reflect a conventional acceptance of the pattern used in most colleges today.

Methods of vitalizing learning. As for the aims toward a "vitalized" liberal education—one which draws its breath from ongoing life rather than from textbooks alone—again the method has come largely to determine the content of the learning. That is, the assumption seems to be, self-education *is* vital education, provided it uses all available devices to relate the learning to the particular student and her present and future life. These devices have been reported in summary form above (page 59). In the actual conduct of the courses, the methods primarily used are *the individual project*—an independent study on some topic, often involving considerable outside-college exploration—; *the group project,* which attempts the same thing on a broader and collaborative basis; roundtable class discussion; and, once more, the *instructor-conference,* to help tie all things up with the student's own general progress. Commenting on the alive spirit in the students which seems to result, the president some years ago wrote:

How does a college accomplish this? The answer is: by changing its basic emphasis from training in scholarship to the development of the individual through as many channels as are fruitful to her.[39]

In the early plan for the college these methods were evidently not thought potent enough by themselves to guarantee vitalizing the whole of the girl's college experience. For some years there was an attempt to "curricularize" not only the subject matter the girl studied but also the college activities she entered and the leisure time that was hers to enjoy. In the case of activities, the girl chose one thing for the year (music, drama, journalism, athletics, etc.); she then joined a weekly two-hour seminar in that activity with other students in her group. A faculty "referee" was present. His role was to advise, not dominate; still, it was stated, "The success of the group activities will depend on the tact, abilities, vision, and enthusiasm of the

[39] C. Warren, "Self-Education: An Experiment," *Progressive Education,* Vol. 11, p. 268, April–May, 1934.

faculty referee." [40] The students were graded on their participation. The aims held out were: development of initiative and skill; leadership; instruction in fundamental principles; and enjoyment.

"Leisure time," which was distinguished from "free time," was provided for daily, during an hour and a half after lunch. Here the girl's only requirement was to keep a record of what she did. For the improvement of her use of leisure time, handicraft rooms, travel and debating groups, book discussions, etc., were made available at that time.

The organization of extra-class activity on this scale continued for some years after the college's founding. Gradually, though, it was felt that such organization did not make school active and vital so much as it made the activities like school. The regimentation of students' time to this degree, moreover, was found to be something of a denial of the individuating principle on which the college was founded.[41] At the present time, activities are handled as informally as at other colleges. Participation in them for the most part is decided by the main study-interest of the students. Since, for instance, drama, music, and art have at Sarah Lawrence (as at the other progressive colleges) full curriculum status, the activities in those fields—"extra-curricular" in traditional schools—tend here to merge indistinguishably with the regular course of study. From "making the activities like school," in other words, the emphasis has swung to making school like activities. (To be sure, in some of the more formal subject-fields, such as history, or philosophy, the transition is not so easy to make, and integrative work of this kind remains to be done.)

Methods of socializing individual education. In the section on primary college aims it was seen that no unusual notice of social-centered aims featured the early Sarah Lawrence program, and that aims of this kind grew gradually within the program, even as in other colleges and in the general social scene, during

[40] M. Coats, "Sarah Lawrence College Statutes of Instruction," p. 11.
[41] Specific mention of the original activities set-up is last mentioned in the 1933–34 catalog.

the depression 'thirties. They were in the earlier years treated conventionally through the usual roster of subjects bearing on social matters. But such courses, not being required, might be taken by only a relative few. Field work, on the other hand, has since provided a type of social experience which, though perhaps limited and transient, is entered into by nearly all. The exploratory courses, some one of which is taken by virtually every freshman, have increased the general use and potency of field work, as is illustrated by Mrs. Raushenbush:

> . . . questions of labor policy, for instance, became very much alive when, during a study of a neighboring community, the girls ran into the local milk company's labor troubles; so did the question of government relief when a student interviewed a courageous, rather disheartened Negro woman who refused to go on relief and preferred to try supporting an unemployed husband and several children on the money she earned as a maid. The housing problem was approached through interviews with people living in low-income houses in the community. The students regularly attended the meetings of a housing group handling the problems in this community; they brought to their visits to the blighted areas previous knowledge of the town, its make-up, its general economy, information about this particular housing problem, and the beginnings, at least, of a technique for getting additional information. Their work led, finally, to a survey by the students for the local housing authority; and their survey formed the basis for the Federal housing project.[42]

Beyond the fair degree of commonness of such types of experience, it is not easy to see at once how the individualized program of each Sarah Lawrence girl can, by any of the specific devices so far reviewed, be made to take on a strongly society-centered outlook. As President Warren herself has said, ". . . developing students who are willing and able to question and analyze their function in a democracy is probably the most difficult task in college teaching." [43]

Two possible aids to a better answer, one from the "extra-curricular" side of the Sarah Lawrence program, present themselves. The first concerns the nature and set-up of the college

---

[42] E. Raushenbush, *Literature for Individual Education*, p. 30.
[43] C. Warren, *A New Design for Women's Education*, p. 182.

community. Although such is outside the province of this discussion, the chance for the girls to learn, at least by analogy, what it means to be part of a self-governing state are ascribed by Miss Doershuck to lie in the following condition:

Each college forms in itself a small community. Its organization must give opportunity for the sharing of responsibility, for free participation and expression. I have referred to the Community Government at Sarah Lawrence College, as based on a constitution in which both faculty and student are on equivalent basis, with an elected central committee of each body, meeting together to consider matters of common concern.[44]

The other possible aid to an answer has risen only during the past (1941–42) school year. Prompted in part by the current emphases on general community solidarity for economy and defense, in part by a longer-time interest of its sponsors in promoting such trends, Sarah Lawrence has organized what is tentatively being called the Institute for Democratic Morale. The aims are stated:

1. To provide the most effective way in which the College and individuals on the faculty can contribute to the present crisis. 2. To provide the most effective way in which students can work actively in the present situation at the same time that they are carrying on their education.[45]

Highlights of the Institute's projected program, some of which has already been in operation during the past year, are:

A series of weekly forums on inter-cultural problems (this series was successfully run, titled "United Nationalities Roundtables")
Consultation on child care and personality problems.
Nutrition exhibits by the science department for college and community.
Agency for advice on consumer problems conducted by faculty, students, and community leaders.
Speakers Bureau open to students and community for training in speaking and group leadership.
Groups in community chorus, orchestra, folk-dancing, recreational leadership.

[44] B. Doershuck, op. cit., p. 114.
[45] "Memorandum on the Sarah Lawrence College Institute for Democratic Morale" (mimeographed), April 24, 1942.

Courses (on democratic and national topics) open to community, students and alumnae.[46]

Students' participation, according to present plans, would be secured through the inclusion of part or all of certain regular courses within the Institute's work; through special projects to be undertaken in conjunction with community people; and through invitation at all times to students to attend the meetings and forums during the year. If such a plan matures, it would seem to show promise of holding decided socializing values. The marriage of the two kinds of values, social and individual, in other words, is no longer thought to be an East is East, West is West proposition. About this the Memorandum on the Institute comments: "Because Sarah Lawrence education has always emphasized field work in the community and here-and-now application of learning, it is exceptionally equipped to fill this particular need."

Evaluation and control.

A review of the methods used by the college, since its founding, for the evaluation and guidance of its students shows a progression, similar to the treatment of study-content, in the discovering of what the implications of an individual program mean. The original plan called for a program of testing similar in nature, if not in form, to that at the conventional college.[47] At the completion of each "goal" in the syllabus, the student could qualify for one of three sets of tests, according to whether she had completed just the work, more than the work, or an original treatment of the work assigned. The tests were to be "objective and standardized."

Partly to show that Sarah Lawrence girls who wished to transfer to senior college elsewhere after their two years were well prepared, a board of examiners from other high-standing colleges tested these students in each subject at the year's end. For two-year graduation from the college, the requirements, commensurate with the college aims of that day, were stated:

[46] *Ibid.*
[47] Information from M. Coats, *op. cit.*

The awarding of the diploma will be conditioned by: a. Mastery of certain courses of study; b. Creditable achievement in group activities; c. Records showing profitable use of time set aside in the daily schedule.[48]

The first few years' experience showed that such kinds of evaluation could not be matched with a program which, as time went on, was becoming more and more nearly unique for each student. Reviewing the first ten years' experience, President Warren writes:

With the clearer understanding experience has given us of the implications of the aims with which the college was established, the basis of evaluation are also gradually clarifying with some insight of what may be factors of the "total development of the student." Criteria of objective, academic, standards of achievement, or of strong initiative or independence may often cause failure to integrate experience with learning in college. On the other hand, irrational motives, interests that appear unreasonable or that conflict with academic duty may be of great importance for constructive guidance and teaching. . . .[49]

The growing awareness of truths like these led to the removal of systematic tests (along with the syllabus-plan) and the substitution of "qualitative" grading, i.e. "an analysis of the student's work in terms of her development" [50]—a process which admittedly was hard and required skill. Yet this in itself was not enough. Clearly, if "irrational motives" should be considered as having weight in the evaluative process, then some means must be devised whereby these irrational motives and other things about the student could be found out. As expressed by Miss Ruth Munroe, "Once we transformed 'meeting the needs of women students' from a pleasing statement in the catalogue to practical educational procedure, the plaint raised . . . became an acute issue: *we do not know what these needs are.*" [51]

Once again, awareness of this fact made it essential to the college that research become a central feature of the program—a

[48] *Sarah Lawrence College Catalog, 1927–28*, p. 17.
[49] C. Warren, "President's Report," 1926–1936, p. 30.
[50] *Ibid.*
[51] R. L. Munroe, *Teaching the Individual*, p. 39. Italics hers.

step in time with the first president's early statement, "It will be primarily a research college." [52] Accordingly, during seven of the last eight years (six of these with the aid of General Education Board funds) a research committee has worked on problems of students' needs and how they can be determined and treated. The chief method (after a first year of experimenting with statistical devices) has been individual psychological analysis.

One outcome of these prolonged activities has been the retention of a staff-member as full-time research worker in the area of student abilities, attitudes, personality needs, etc.[53] Her findings, in turn, are directly used by the Student Work Committee, a group of four teachers plus the Director of Admissions and the Director of Education, whose function it is to formulate academic policy, review programs, evaluate student-development, and make decisions as to student-classification, diploma, and degree. In matters affecting a particular student, the don of this student becomes temporarily a seventh member of the committee, with voting power.[54] The result of this set-up is that all types of information about the girl, academic and personal, flow into the same clearing house, and may be resorted to simultaneously in each individual case.

The above machinery has been reviewed to show the structure which exists at Sarah Lawrence to make a qualitative student-evaluation, a system which tries to take in "all aspects of the girl's growth" possible. In the words of one officer, "The student, as a whole, becomes the educational unit of the college." With this set-up the following formal periods and types of evaluation are used:

Four times a year each girl's instructors submit short subjective evaluations of her work (usually a paragraph in length), which are reviewed by the Director of Education and then combined into a written report to the girl.

[52] M. Coats, *op. cit.*, p. 2.
[53] For personality diagnosis, for instance, a modified-form of Rorschach Ink-Blot Test is extensively used.
[54] *Sarah Lawrence College*, "Faculty By-Laws, revised as of June, 1941" (mimeographed).

The don submits quarterly reviews of his donnee's work, based partly upon her own "work-records" (quantitative reports of work done) which he has received monthly from her.

At the end of the year, plus these reviews, the instructors submit rating-scale evaluations of their student's ability, attitudes, effort, promise, etc., compared with her own and with normal college expectancy.

In the spring of the year each girl submits a report of plans and study-intentions for the following year.

On the basis of the foregoing evidence, plus other facts at its disposal, The Committee on Student Work "reviews the progress of each student and makes a recommendation at the end of each year with reference to the desirability of further college work for her, to her qualifications for a two-year diploma, or for the A.B. degree." [55]

The present evaluational procedure at Sarah Lawrence, in other words, works to match the *qualitative educational aims* of the college, by watching over the girl's progress from entrance to graduation without the necessary use of a single test or arithmetic figure—although these may, in any individual case warranting it, be employed.

Admissions policies.

Concerning this final section of the review of the Sarah Lawrence educational program, only one important change need be noted.

The college was founded, it has been seen, to be an experiment in liberal arts education. An element in this experiment, originally, was to be the nature of the clientele. As a two-year college, Sarah Lawrence was designed to deal with the girl who did not want four years of higher education, especially four years of the hyper-academic brand that was then felt to be prevalent. The first page of the Statutes of 1927 makes this clear:

Sarah Lawrence College was founded with the idea that it should give a new type of college education to a carefully selected group of students . . . (girls) who do not fit readily into the training of scholarly minds which is the chief task of the established college.

[55] *Sarah Lawrence College Catalog, 1941–42*, p. 54.

. . . There have been few attempts to work out on the college level the type of education best adapted to the needs of such students.[56]

Acting upon such ideas, the first catalog stated that the college was either for the girl best in social spirit and leadership, whose goal was "sound scholarship rather than high academic rating, and whose major interest is in group activities"; [57] or for the student who showed marked talent in art, music, or dramatics.[58]

Whether the foregoing criteria proved too restrictive, or impracticable in other ways, these criteria quickly faded from the official scene. Writing in the *Nation* in 1930, President Warren listed as requisites for entrance into the college: "Sufficient intellectual capacity; desire for independent work; and enough maturity for social responsibility." [59] (There is no mention of special interests or "extra-curricular" promise in catalogs after the first issue.) These criteria have stayed virtually unchanged to the present day. The summary of these qualities is now given, "In short, the college selects from among the applicants for admission those students who give promise of being ready to profit most from working in the environment which it provides." [60]

The present implication, in other words, is that Sarah Lawrence, as a four-year college granting the B.A. degree, offers a program suitable for the normal applicant to any first-rank college, provided she is prepared to assume the added active role in her education which Sarah Lawrence requires. As has been seen above, the experimental features of the program have increased rather than fallen off, and there seems no reason to think this change toward the norm in admissions policy has signaled a turn to an educational pattern more like the other four-year colleges. Rather, the policy would seem to say that though the content and method of the Sarah Lawrence girl's

---

[56] M. Coats, *op. cit.*, p. 1.
[57] *Sarah Lawrence College Catalog, 1927–28*, p. 17.
[58] cf. the early Bennington requirements, Chapter IV, this study.
[59] Warren, *op. cit.*, p. 550.
[60] *Sarah Lawrence College Catalog, 1941–42*, p. 56.

education will differ from the content and method at other colleges (as, indeed, it does to some degree at all colleges), the long-
range purpose and reference are, at base, common to them all.
As a recent Sarah Lawrence book says:

> Our major effort can be described simply. We are trying to edu-
> cate our students to be normal, functioning people in a world in
> which they should take an active part—a more intelligent part, per-
> haps, because of their training here. We want them to understand
> that the kind of world they are to live in will be determined at least
> to some degree by the values they have and the wisdom they can
> achieve. We want them to know in any case that a world worth liv-
> ing in is not to be had for the asking, but must be constantly guarded
> and continually re-made, and we want to give them the knowledge
> and understanding that will help them take their part in this con-
> tinuous process.[61]

CONCLUSION

Sarah Lawrence College was founded to be a venture in
higher education which might capitalize and carry on the educational lessons which had been developing in the progressive
elementary and secondary schools.[62] As that kind of venture, it
is committed to an experimental philosophy of its job. For this
reason, no review of trends in its program (and much, including
most of the personnel policy, has been left out here) can safely
conclude without emphasizing that what has been described is
a moving and changing picture. At present, for instance, discussions are going on regarding the question, "Granted the
primacy of the individual as the educational unit, is it not possible to arrange the successive years of her program on a somewhat more systematic basis, from the standpoint of what she is

[61] E. Raushenbush, *Literature for Individual Education*, p. 4.
[62] Reference here to sample statements made by each president may serve to
illustrate this fairly obvious truth. In her "Statutes of Instruction" (1927), p. 1,
President Coats said the college would be a boon to the progressive schools
because, "As matters stand, such progressive schools . . . admit they revert to
type and put the student through the usual routine preparation as soon as they
come within two or three years of college."
President Warren, in her *Nation* article (1930), "The Sarah Lawrence Plan,"
p. 549, said, "It is attempting to put into practice, on the college level, principles
of education long tested in the best so-called progressive schools."

given a chance to learn?" It can only be predicted that, whatever the outcome of this or other discussions, they will be made the basis for still further experimentation on the question of educating the individual at Sarah Lawrence in the present times.

Chapter IV

The Bennington Program

THE progress of experimental college education in America has been hampered in the past by the simple failure of some of the experiments and their results to reach the public's eyes and ears. All too often it has been a case of the rose "born to blush unseen, and waste its fragrance on the desert air." In recent years, the opposite has begun to be true. Thanks in some part to the growth of systematic college educational literature, but probably more to the increased public interest in higher education, new college ventures, in many cases, have become news. Among such cases, something of a prodigy is Bennington.

Some of this, in turn, may have been due to the long wait that ensued between the first official notice of the college and its actual opening: to wit, nine years. In 1923 a group of residents of Old Bennington and North Bennington, Vermont, first connected contemporary opinions of educators about the shortage of college facilities for New England girls with an idea to start a college for women in their own locale.[1] Under the leadership of Dr. Vincent Ravi-Booth, a minister in that region, and with the assistance of several others, notably Mr. and Mrs. H. P. McCullough, the group instigated a series of meetings with educators of the Northeast, climaxed by a general meeting at the Colony Club in New York City, April 28, 1924. The wide-

[1] Material for this historical summary from *The Educational Plan for Bennington College;* from P. D. Schillp (ed.), *Higher Education Faces the Future,* chapter on Bennington by R. D. Leigh; from R. D. Leigh, "Bennington Gets Under Way," *Progressive Education,* Vol. 9, pp. 370–372, September, 1932; and from W. Fowlie, "The Bennington Experiment," *The French Review,* Vol. 11, pp. 93–101, December, 1937.

spread interest already built up is attested by the number present, variously estimated at between three hundred and five hundred. President Comstock of Radcliffe served as chairman. President Nielson of Smith spoke of the need for a new women's college, based upon experimental ideas, in New England. Dr. W. H. Kilpatrick presented the broad outlines for such a base, in a talk entitled "Why a New Plan?" [2] Some discussion followed. Dr. Ravi-Booth described the proposed site. The meeting ended with the passing of a resolution:

> *Resolved,* that we cordially endorse the proposed plans for the college for women at Old Bennington, Vermont, as presented to us this evening, and commend the enterprise to the very favorable consideration of all concerned.[3]

The organization of the college proceeded slowly and carefully. In 1925 a charter was granted by Vermont to "The Bennington College Corporation," and a board of trustees was formed. Two educational conferences in that year defined the goal as that of "a highly qualitative experiment in 'progressive education' in the college field, with a curriculum adapted to the actual needs of young women in the modern world." [4] Fodder for the development of the program was presented to the trustees the next year in the form of a field-study report by Miss Amy Kelly, then of Wellesley College, on college education in Europe and the United States. The actual program, however, was developed after January, 1928, following the election by the trustees of Robert D. Leigh, of the Government Department at Williams, as president of the as-yet-non-existent college. Using all the evidence on college education which he and others had collected, Dr. Leigh produced, late in 1928, *The Educational Plan for Bennington College.* This document in its 1931 revised edition defined almost completely the program of the college as it operated during its first ten years.

The opening of Bennington was delayed by money-raising

---

[2] "Addresses Delivered at the Colony Club, New York City" (mimeographed manuscript in the possession of Dr. Kilpatrick), April 28, 1924.

[3] *Ibid.*

[4] R. D. Leigh, "Bennington Gets Under Way," *op. cit.,* p. 370.

difficulties, as a result of the 1929 financial crash. Original hopes for a four-million-dollar venture had to be replaced by a working figure of a million and a quarter, a change which required a revised tuition policy and some compromises in building construction. The college opened its doors to students in September, 1932. Yet throughout the preparatory nine years, professional and popular interest had been kept high; [5] this fact is borne out by Bennington's enviable feat of being able to select its first class of eighty girls from over two hundred applications.

Since 1936, the year that this first class completed its four-year course, the college has awarded the A.B. degree, usually at the end of four years of college study.

In 1941 Dr. Leigh, fulfilling an intention made known when he first assumed the position, resigned the Presidency and was succeeded by Lewis W. Jones, an original member of the Bennington faculty in the Social Studies Division. In this year, also, Dr. Alvin C. Eurich and staff completed an on-location evaluative study of the first nine years of the college's operation.

Primary college aims.

The development of the aims of Bennington College, from the first ideas of its starters in 1923 to the issue of the first catalog in 1932, traces an interesting course from a vague and general felt need through stages of crystallization down to an eventual creed of ten educational points. This course is all the more interesting because, since it has kept a surprising consistency, it can be rather clearly followed.

The first wishes of Dr. Ravi-Booth and his group at Old Bennington are stated to have been for a college that would embody "a departure in undergraduate education in line with best modern standards and insight," [6] which would nevertheless also

---

[5] At the ground-breaking ceremonies at North Bennington, August 7, 1931, for instance, over a thousand were present, including Governor Wilson of Vermont; President Garfield of Williams; President Nielson of Smith, who spoke; Robert Frost, who read a poem; and Dorothy Canfield Fisher. *School and Society*, Vol. 34, p. 223, August 15, 1931.

[6] *The Educational Plan for Bennington College*, p. 4.

maintain "standards at least equal to those of the best American colleges for women." [7] A year of intermittent discussion on this basis ended in the aforementioned Colony Club meeting of April, 1924.

At the Colony Club meeting the aims for the college, as a result of Dr. Nielson's and Dr. Kilpatrick's talks, took on the beginnings of definition. The former called for a college which might avoid the planlessness of most contemporary colleges, and for a woman's college which would no longer bind women's education to trying to prove that women can learn what a man can learn:

> This attitude that was forced upon them in the beginning has led them to be rather more conservative than the men's colleges, since there are still some groups of people who do not know that it has been proved, a thousand times over, that women can stand all the boys are getting, and perhaps more.[8]

Dr. Kilpatrick, proceeding from this standpoint, called for a college built upon three pillars: [9] (1) A cultural college of the first grade. (2) A college which might use as little as possible of mere tradition, and as much as possible "a conscientious, scientific effort to adopt methods to solve the problems as they come up." (3) An "honest and stubborn effort at the founding to leave the future control of the institution to the best thought of the future." These "pillars" the speaker brought together in his concluding paragraph:

> We are at the end of one epoch in the education of women. A new epoch is long since overdue. The new scientific principle of education, already applied to elementary and secondary education, should now be applied to higher education; and a conscientious, scientific study of the whole problem is what we propose.

In the year following the Colony Club meeting, the conferences on Bennington College (as has been noted above) identified the goal of the college with the progressive education

[7] *Bennington College*, "Announcement for the first year, 1932–1933," p. 3.
[8] "Addresses Delivered at the Colony Club, New York City," April 28, 1924.
[9] *Ibid.*

movement. President Leigh, from his earliest writings on, seized upon this identification as the chief *raison d'être,* from the standpoint of American education, for Bennington College. In his mind the college's big opportunity lay in doing what Dr. Kilpatrick had called on it to do: apply the newest educational principles, already at work in grade and high schools, at the college level; or, in his words,

> The significance of the Bennington program is that, by adding a final link in the chain of "progressive" institutions, it makes possible on a small scale a schooling based on modern educational concepts from the nursery school through the end of formal education.[10]

If the joining of the college to the chain of progressive educational institutions in America can be called a blanket aim of Bennington College, it follows that the specific aims for the college, as they evolved, should have shown a decided closeness to the aims being developed in progressive elementary and secondary schools of the time. They should have shown closeness also to the ideas of contemporary advocates for college reform in a "progressive" direction—ideas which for the most part were still not finding favorable college localities for action. The effect upon the developing Bennington program is described by Leigh:

> More than has usually been the case, this plan is a group product rather than a personal formulation. Whatever individuality it may have possessed four years ago has been hopelessly lost in the natural give-and-take of educational ideas since that time.[11] (He cites Dean Max McConn's general proposals in an earlier article [12] as "an almost exact description of the underlying philosophy and administration of Bennington College.")

Whatever the general pool of ideas which supplied the source for Bennington's aims, the eventual formulation was an educational creed of ten points, which appeared in the first catalog (1932–1933) and has continued through to the latest issue (1941–

[10] R. D. Leigh, "Bennington Gets Under Way," *op. cit.,* p. 371.
[11] *Ibid.*
[12] M. McConn, "The Problem of Interest at the College Level," *Progressive Education,* Vol. 8, pp. 680–684, December, 1931.

1942) without the deletion or addition of a single point, and with change in only a handful of the words. In a sense, the use of the term "aims" is misleading, since this creed is perhaps more a statement of the college's beliefs and policies about the educational process than a proposal of goals toward which it hopes to continue moving. (The catalog itself calls them "ideas underlying the educational program.") For the sake of comparison with the other two colleges, however, the list is given here *in toto;* from this it may then be possible to draw out those which serve as the principal "directional aims" for the student's education, leaving the "working aims" for the subsequent discussion on actual methods which have arisen at the college during its ten years of operation.

The aims for Bennington College as of 1941–1942 are stated in the catalog as follows:

(1) that education is a process continuing through life, persisting most effectively in the years after college when the habit of educating oneself has been acquired;

(2) that the College should accustom its students to the habit of engaging voluntarily in learning rather than of submitting involuntarily at certain periods to formal instruction;

(3) that such educational self-dependence can be developed most effectively if the student works at tasks which have meaning and interest for her;

(4) that continuing education, self-initiated, is most likely to take place where the student has attained expertness, or a sense of mastery in a few fields of enduring interest or use, rather than smatterings in a great many fields;

(5) that external disciplines, such as compulsory class attendance, competitive and publicly awarded grades and prizes, periodic written examinations on formalized blocks of knowledge, and numerical accumulation of credits to earn degrees, interfere seriously with real incentives and internal disciplines related to the student's own developing purposes and interests;

(6) that direct experiences—planning, organizing, manipulating, constructing and investigating, in conjunction with reading and the acquisition of knowledge—are valuable means for developing permanent interests pursued voluntarily;

(7) that tools of learning such as statistics, and the use of English, to have meaning as well as to be most economically mastered, should

be connected immediately, or in the process of learning, with the ends for which they are instruments rather than acquired as separate disciplines related vaguely to possible distant use;

(8) that programs of college work should at all points allow for the fact that between different students and in the same student at different times there is wide individual variation in the subject matter or problems which have sufficient meaning to engage the student in active learning leading to understanding;

(9) that intellectual development cannot and should not be isolated from the development of the whole personality, and that general arrangements, and especially individual guidance, should give proper weight not only to intellectual factors in personal growth, but also to physical, emotional, moral, and aesthetic factors as well;

(10) that the College should accept responsibility for cultivating in its students by all available means attitudes of social cooperation, participation and responsibility, rather than aloofness; a sympathetic but objective and realistic understanding of the world of our own day as well as a sense of perspective derived from an understanding of the past; an attitude of suspended judgment towards the strange and the new, and tolerance toward people and customs alien to the student's own experience.[13]

Digesting the above creed in terms of objectives for the student (and leaving out points 4, 5, and 7 as matters of teaching policy, to be discussed further on), it becomes possible to arrive at the following focal points for the Bennington aims for the first ten years:

1. Education for each student should in content and method be continuous with *life,* and especially *her* life (points 1, 3, 6, and 9).

2. The educational pattern for each student should literally be defined and motivated by her own individual wants, needs, traits, and abilities (points 2, 3, and 8).

3. Such a vital and individual-centered education is not enough until it helps prepare her for intelligent, cooperative living in her society (point 10).

It becomes evident, in other words, that the stated aims for Bennington College in its first ten years, when reduced to common denominators, emerge sounding very much like those

[13] *Bennington College Bulletin,* "Announcement for the Year 1941–1942," pp. 6–7.

evolved (independently, of course) for Sarah Lawrence during its own first decade. As in the case of that college, it should now be seen what methods at Bennington have characterized the working-out of these aims.

The course and method of study.

The Bennington educational plan, it has been noted, was "hatched" over a period of nine years. During that time, it had a chance to absorb the nutriment of advice from many of the best educational minds of the country; and its president took pains to capitalize this chance.[14] Yet no plan can foresee all things; and the dynamics of actually putting it into motion, affected as they must be by all local factors of time, situation, and personalities, often bring great changes within a short period. At Bennington the changes in over-all policy, up to 1942, have not been especially great (in fact, in many ways they have been remarkably small); still they are worthy of consideration. For this reason the discussion of methods is split into two main time-divisions: "the preparatory years," 1923 to 1932; and "the college years," 1932 to 1942. (The changes inaugurated in the fall of 1942 by the new administration will be treated in a separate, later section.) This division, however, for the sake of analysis will be repeated under three headings of "methods," in keeping with the categories used in the Sarah Lawrence analysis above: namely, (a) methods of individual study; (b) methods of vitalizing learning; and (c) methods of socializing individual education. (These three categories, it may not need to be restated, derive from the three main classes of aims discovered at the colleges under study.)

a. Methods of individual study.

Preparatory years. Although the developing of the Bennington program was shared in by many professional minds to the

[14] *The Educational Plan for Bennington College,* for instance, was sent to numbers of prominent educators for comment and criticism. The 1931 edition of the Plan quotes approving comments from sixty-four of those solicited—men and women almost universally possessed of a national reputation in education or an allied profession.

unusual extent noted above, direct responsibility for designing the plan's base and for evolving the actual details must go respectively to two men: William H. Kilpatrick of Teachers College, Columbia University (who also served as Chairman of the Board of Trustees from 1931 until 1938), and Robert Leigh, the first president.

In his speech at the Colony Club in 1924, the former went beyond the matter of broad aims for the new college, to propose five points of innovating policy. Three of these had to do with fitting the educational pattern more truly to the individual seeker. Dr. Kilpatrick petitioned the Bennington-to-be: to make "a very much more careful study of each individual student to find out how to advance that student not only in the course of knowledge, but in regards to his vocation afterwards"; to create a new deal on required courses, giving no course "required for mental training value"; and to make sure that the content of the courses was evolved "for the sake of the student and not for the sake of the subjects." [15]

In President Leigh's master-document, *The Educational Plan for Bennington College,* issued more than four years later, these features, with implementing details, were conspicuously present. Point number four of his list of eighteen "Essential Features of the Bennington Program," after the mention of admission, tuition, and scholarship policies, was given:

Individu'ally arranged work for the first two years taking full account of previous school courses and of differences in personal development and interest, instead of general requirements or free election of courses.[16]

The text of the Plan, in its description of student work for the first two years, elaborated upon this:

. . . the work for this period will be individually arranged by deliberate conference between college officers and each student. This should not be taken to mean an unrestricted elective system; the

[15] "Addresses Delivered at the Colony Club," Why a New Plan? by W. H. Kilpatrick.
[16] *Op. cit.,* p. 3.

student's program is to be based upon a careful analysis of her present needs, aptitudes, and interests. . . .[17]

How far such individualizing at that time was intended to go
beyond the individual selection of courses is not clear from this
or other early statements. The impression gained, interestingly
enough, is that originally it was not meant to go very far *in the
first two years* of the student's course. The latter two years, to
be sure, were planned to be "similar in aim and method to
honors type of work now open to selected students in several
existing colleges"; [18] and the description of methods to be used
in those years mentions all the study-freedom that is now typical
of all four years at the college. But the program for the first two
years was then outlined to consist of four fairly conventional introductory courses, plus "the equivalent of a fifth course known
as the trial major conference" [19] (plus also any "tool courses,"
such as mathematics or foreign languages, which might be
deemed necessary to the particular student's advanced work).
Of the trial major conference more, shortly, must be said. Sufficient to say now, it was from the first planned to aid the individual explore her study interests; but it was also originally
planned to be a group, not an individual activity.

Thus most of the pattern of study for the Junior Division,
according to this initial plan, centered around a normal procedure of course-taking. What individualizing methods of instruction the teachers themselves might use was not specified.

The proposed content for those introductory courses, moreover, shows a central feature which, as a something originally
planned for Bennington, may come as a considerable surprise.
This feature concerns an intention to mold the first-two-year
course-taking into a pattern of experience quite similar to the
plans used by other contemporary colleges to give a "general
education" (*v.* Chapter II, this study). *The Educational Plan*
states it:

[17] *Ibid.,* p. 9.
[18] *Ibid.,* p. 3.
[19] *Ibid.,* p. 10.

In the work of the first two years an effort will be made, so far as is practicable, to correlate the four courses round a cultural epoch. It is planned to have the general subject of the first year, or even first two years, an attempt to understand modern western civilization—its literature, its art, its political, economic, and scientific base.[20, 21]

Later on in the document, President Leigh made this intent event more explicit:

The breadth of outlook which has always been associated with the liberal college will be sought at Bennington in more than one way. Either during her school years or during her first college years each student will be introduced to the major fields of human achievement as a prerequisite to the intelligent choice of the field of concentration.[22]

What happened to crowd out this particular working aim, between the time of its formulation and the current operation of the college, is a question which has no documentary answer, although doubtless individuals at the college could informally explain. In general, it may be suspected that such a blanket requirement was found difficult to work into a college which had set itself out first and foremost to build its program around the individual girl. More concretely, however, it seems probable that the culture-orientation plans were doomed to be overshadowed by yet another feature of the original program.

This feature may be presented as the last and most important method towards individual study, as proposed in the pre-college *Educational Plan*. It appears in several places in that document, showing itself with complete consistency in the sections dealing respectively with admissions, method of study, the awarding of the degree, etc. In the section under discussion here, it is stated: [23]

[20] *Ibid.*

[21] In the next to the last page of the *Plan*, a statement by Professor R. B. Perry in *The Harvard Alumni Bulletin*, January 23, 1930, quoted there, points out that Bennington's first two years (as planned then) combined "features taken from the so-called 'orientation courses' with the Meiklejohn idea (at Wisconsin) of relating them to the culture of an epoch."

[22] *Ibid.*, p. 12.

[23] *Ibid.*, p. 9.

The primary objective set clearly before every student immediately upon entrance is *to discover for herself the field of human achievement in which she possesses a marked interest combined with distinct competence.*[24] The general pattern of work for the first two years will be designed to aid her in this quest.

What each girl achieves in her later college years after finding her proper "field of human achievement" has come to attract a large percentage of the widespread attention that has been paid the Bennington program. Whether the original *Plan* intended this to take on such proportions as it has cannot be known. Certainly, however, large stress was from the first put on the factor of intensive, specialized study. From such study, especially during the latter two years—the Senior Division, as it was called from the first—the principal dynamics of individualized work, characterizing the college as a whole, were expected to spring.

To return, moreover, to the problem of the first two years, one implied aim of the introductory courses for that period has been quoted as that of preparing the student for an intelligent choice of a major field. This is made pre-eminent in the later statement by the *Plan* (p. 10): "The specific object of the introductory courses is the exploration of the various major fields to discover permanent interests and competence." It may be argued that to reconcile, in teaching, this "specific object" with the "general object" of orienting the student to western civilization is after all perfectly feasible. The fact remains, in the ensuing operation of the college, the "orienting" aim rather quickly disappeared from the foreground of the Bennington program, while the preoccupation of the student's time with the development of her major study (to the best of available evidence, discussed below) rapidly grew.

To summarize these foregoing first facts about Bennington instructional methods, then, the early plans for the college stressed a program built upon the uniqueness of each individual problem. This stress, however, did not at that time mean plans for large-scale individuation of the content of study in

[24] Italics mine.

the first two years. Rather this period was then seen as a time for an introduction to all major fields of learning, and an orientation to western culture in general. Yet, more concretely, the Junior Division was also planned as *a time for discovering the girl's proper field for concentrated study on an advanced, free basis in the upper two years;* and this drive toward specialization received the major share of attention. It came to be the feature which chiefly identified the program of the prospective new college.

College years. To attempt an analysis of a college's workings from the outside, it has been frequently pointed out in this study, is a process racked by limitations. Many of the "choices and changes" most vital to the college program either do not find their way into the available literature or are reported with small hint of the real factors behind the choice or change.

In the case of Bennington, signs of outward change in the program for the first ten years have been quite few. Yet the decided changes being put into effect in 1942 are manifestly a result of developments that happened during that first decade. In order to come closer to what some of these developments have been, it will be necessary at times to use evidence from sources not at present publicly available. Some of this comes from recorded studies and interviews as yet unpublished; some comes from direct conversation with college officers, and must run the risk of being judged as hearsay. In all cases, however, the correctness of the evidence may to some extent be checked by the outward, announced changes which that evidence has underlain. Whether the underlying evidence and the outward changes really do relate to one another is a matter on which the writer's analysis itself must be judged.

Discussions at Bennington of the first decade of the college popularly make a distinction between the "early years" and the "later years." This is used not to refer to any particular time-division so much as to indicate the extremes of a period of gradual change. For the sake of throwing those changes into relief, the same convention will be used here.

In the early years, then, of the college after its opening in 1932, methods having to do with individual study saw two major points of change from the original *Educational Plan*. One of these was an increasing emphasis upon the trial-major conference. The other, companion, change was the informalizing of the course-plan for the first two as well as the latter two years.

The trial-major conference had been projected in the precollege *Educational Plan* as "an informal group attached to each of the introductory courses." It was believed that the courses themselves would provide for the greater part of the student's exploration of fields toward a major area of concentration. The trial-major conference, selected in some one field by the entering student after counsel from her advisers, was to serve additionally to "carry the student as rapidly as possible into the more individual and informal methods characteristic of the last two college years." [25] It was scheduled to occupy about one-fifth of the student's working time.

By the time the college opened, it was seen that for some girls a systematic two years of study in different fields mainly for the sake of exploration to find a major interest was a waste of time; these girls already knew what they wanted to do. Thus it was specified:

> When, however, a student at entrance has a serious specialized interest and a desire to concentrate immediately the trial major conference group may be enlarged in scope and character so as to include two-fifths, three-fifths, and even more of her time and effort.[26]

Whether the example of these students led others to ask for the same privilege, or whether it proved too hard to tell students with "a serious, specialized interest" from those who temporarily thought they had one, the swelling in the proportion of work done on the trial-major specialty soon became general. In the third year of the college the percentage of time allowed for the trial-major conference was officially changed from "one-fifth or more" of the student's working hours to "one-fourth or

[25] *The Educational Plan for the Bennington College*, p. 10.
[26] *Bennington College*, "Announcement for the First Year," p. 7.

more." At the same time, the method was stated no longer as an out-and-out group activity but as work "conducted by means of individual or group conferences or both." [27] Actually, the individual tutorial soon became by all odds the prevailing technique. Evidence points, in other words, to the fact that the gap in idea and method between the Junior and the Senior Division was early and rather decidedly narrowed. The gap that did remain was indicated in the fact that the Junior Division student was expected to change her major when desiring to do so, and to keep up her exploration of other fields with the possibility of this in mind.

The introductory courses, meanwhile, retreated correspondingly from the focus of the student's attention. The idea that they should join in a pattern to present a "cultural epoch," as has been noted, gradually passed from the scene. The catalogs continued to say,[28] "In so far as they are organized around definite historical periods the introductory groups concern themselves with modern civilization . . ."; but this was followed, a few sentences later, by the qualification:

The choice of content from the modern world is a secondary rather than a primary principle of organizing the work of the Junior Division. . . . Some groups are not organized around historical periods at all.

With the decline of the "cultural orientation" aims and with the spread of early concentration on the trial-major, thus playing down the need for exploratory work, the two chief reasons for taking a pattern of several introductory courses were weakened if not removed. The result was that, to a certain extent, the original plan became reversed: that is, the introductory course, along with other course-work, actually tended toward becoming the appendage of the trial-major conference. For all four years in the college, the pattern became a concentration upon a specialized study, filled out by whatever introductory courses and "workshop" activity ("tool courses," or special technical work) in that field might be prescribed; and balanced to a

[27] *Bennington College*, "Announcement for the Third Year, 1934–1935," p. 13.
[28] *Ibid.*, p. 12.

varying degree by work in other introductory courses, or informally arranged instruction [29] in other fields.

The effect of this growth of intensive, specialized work on the college scene was to create a veritable hive of independent activity, wherein the terms "courses" and "hours" often had little formal place. As a contemporary writer describes it,

> There is no rigidity in the curriculum. The new student, to her bewilderment, finds nothing fixed and prescribed. She must make choices. She has counsel available, but the decision is hers. She does not take courses, she makes them.[30]

The early years of the college, in other words, quickly moved toward a fulfillment of the primary working aim held out to prospective students before Bennington's opening: "Your degree will be given on the basis of a demonstration that you have learned how to stand on your own feet and to work with skill and understanding in your chosen field." [31] The strength of this aim was evidently great enough so that it came to govern the content and method of study not only for the upper division, but for all of the four college years.

The "later years" at Bennington have seen not so much a change from this situation as a development of it. The distinction between the major and the trial-major, besides the matter of different college years, continued to lessen. Although provision for a fairly easy change in the trial-majors was officially retained, with the stated note of encouragement,[32] "Such changes are frequently made, in accordance with the exploratory purpose of Junior Division work," instructors report that in practice more than one such change for each student was unusual. The work of the trial-major student tended to grow only slightly less advanced than that of her Senior Division counterpart.

Such a stepping-up of the Junior Division student's trial-major work has been accompanied by two further changes which

[29] Two students in Bennington's first class, for instance, went to an instructor with an interest in reading Dante. The work of the three of them in this area constituted a "course" which lasted for more than two years.

[30] H. C. Herring, "Bennington," *Nation*, Vol. 137, p. 651, December 6, 1933.

[31] *The Educational Plan for Bennington College*, p. 6. See discussion of *Evaluation*, below.

[32] *Bennington College*, "Announcement for the Sixth Year, 1937–1938," p. 13.

may or may not bear causal relations. Along with the accentuation of the trial-major there grew an increased emphasis upon the academic Division as the administrative unit of the educational program. Originally (1932) there had been four of these: Art and Music; [33] Literature; Social Studies; and Science. With some changes in wording, these persisted until 1936. In that year,[34] "for administrative purposes and convenience" the four divisions were organized as seven "major groups." The latter three divisions stayed the same, while art-and-music (or "Art," as the division had come to be called) was subdivided into four major groups: art, drama, dance, and music. For all administrative purposes, these seven groups functioned as autonomous divisions, arranging curricula, passing on student records, etc., until 1940.[35] At this time, another adjustment in the arts division produced three major groups: art; "drama-dance-design" (renamed "theatre arts" the next year); and music.

The impact, upon the students, of these several splittings was to create a certain air of separate academic schools under one college roof, and to raise, rather than lower, interdivisional walls. This appears bound to have made some problem out of the announced college aim, "The plan of work is . . . designed to broaden interests as well as to give some degree of specialized competence. . . ." [36] Within each division, moreover, as these grew in supervisory importance, *general standards for content of study and performance* were built up—a thing which at times seems to have threatened the creed of individuality to which the college is officially committed.[37]

---

[33] The Arts at Bennington, as in the other progressive colleges, have full status as members of the curriculum.

[34] *Bennington College,* "Announcement for the Fifth Year, 1936–1937," p. 27.

[35] It is true that the Junior Division student is officially under the administration of her counselor and the Committee on Student Personnel, though her work is "supervised by the major teaching groups." However, since her counselor (up till now) is usually the teacher of her trial-major conference, the natural tie-up with the major group representing her field can be seen.

[36] *Bennington College, op. cit.,* p. 18.

[37] F. F. Park, "A Study of the Junior Division," 1937–1938 (mimeographed). This unpublished study finds, after extensive faculty interviews, that the divisions seemed to range in the matter of organization of study-content, from one which gave a completely worked-out hierarchy of study, in terms of the subject-field, to another which frankly stated, "A basic content has not been worked out."

Another result of the growth in divisional organization of courses and work-standards was to reduce the amount of course-work within a major group which might be profitably taken by a student majoring in an outside division. Since more and more of each division's work became dependent upon a background of experience and built-up competence in that division, there tended to be less and less open to the average outside student, beyond the division's introductory courses.

In the early years of the college, needs of the non-major student were often met by a semi-formal tutorial or special group, organized more or less spontaneously by teacher and students, on the initiative of either (see, for illustration, footnote 29, p. 89). After the first few experimental years, however, inevitable grooving of some of these *ad hoc* creations occurred. In the words of one instructor, "Teachers grew fond of courses"; and entering students, hearing from their older associates about "Mr. So-and-so's marvelous course in Such-and-such," helped the grooving tendencies by demanding a repeat performance. Consequently there was a gradual absorbing of these earlier experiments into the regularly constituted hierarchy of courses within each division.

All these moves led to the growing up of a certain degree of academic self-sufficiency within the several divisions. The resulting concentration of the student's time within one general field has, perhaps, been the factor which has enabled Bennington Senior Division students to do pieces of work often said to be on a graduate-research level.

In the Junior Division, the declining importance placed on a coverage of the several fields via introductory courses meant the passing of one official device for requiring a general breadth of subject-matter experience (although all students do still take varying numbers of these courses). This has to some degree been compensated by the broadening of the function of the trial-major conference, as well as the subject-matter included in it. In some cases, the conference has been made to amount in itself to a sort of "introductory course" to all sorts of subject matter, through the medium of the trial-major subject—thus serving as a real (and educationally interesting) device toward the integration of acquired knowledge. One teacher defined its general purpose as "The co-ordinating of material from all phases of the student's experience; special criticism of projects, etc.; discussion of plans and personal problems." [38] The conference likewise, however, has been variously interpreted by different teachers in different student cases.

To summarize this section of the discussion, the Bennington program up to the present date shows a ten-year evolution of methods evolved to meet the primary aim of preparing the individual to work intelligently in some field of study for which she is best suited. The individuation of study content has been seen at the college principally in this reference. Outside courses and fields have been advised from time to time to suit individual preference, ability, and need (as usually defined by her major study), rather than as a general prescription. The work in the major field has varied in scope and intensity, in both the Junior and the Senior Division. Where breadth in study has been the working aim (depending upon the individual teacher and the student), its attainment has been made easier by college methods of individual study originated for that purpose: frequent use of tutorials, in major, trial-major, and elsewhere; informally arranged short-term instruction almost at student will; large-scale independence for the student in project and paper work; in short, a philosophy that the facilities of the college are to be used by the student where, when, and in the manner that her purpose (backed up by her counselor) seems to require.

The approach toward broad and meaningful study has also been promoted by certain attitudes of the Bennington program, in sympathy with the progressive movement in education, toward what should constitute the content of subject-matter and learning in the present day. This in itself needs a section for treatment.

[38] F. F. Park, *op. cit.*, p. 2.

b. *Methods of vitalizing learning.*

In the discussion of the actual teaching methods at Sarah Lawrence it was found hard to separate, even for study-purposes, methods for individual study from methods for "vitalized" study. In terms of handling the student, both seem to amount operationally to the same thing—that is, fitting her educational pattern so closely to herself that she feels its relation to her own life and personality.

The methods of organizing and handling the subject matter, however, so that it too bears relation to life, is a matter which carries the discussion into different grounds.

The text of *The Educational Plan for Bennington College* directed itself primarily toward describing a program built around individual scholarship in a major field. Nevertheless there is considerable evidence that the nature of both the scholarship and the major field was to be different from that in the typical college. Like the teaching, the students, and the institution, it was to be more "vital." Four channels of approach toward such a vitality may be cited in the *Plan*: (1) approaches to the unification of knowledge; (2) inclusion of "activities" within the curriculum; (3) attitude toward vocational preparation; (4) the Winter Field Period.

(1) Approaches to the unification of knowledge.

Preparatory years. In Dr. Kilpatrick's ground-clearing speech, "Why a New Plan?," at the Colony Club in 1924, the second of five points about desired innovations in the college program was stated:

We wish, I think, a new deal in the consideration of certain administrative features. I wish to question the prevailing American notion, the splitting up of education into little pieces, into so many bricks, to be fitted together afterwards and made into an education. . . .[39]

In a spirit continuous with this, the *Plan* made it plain that

[39] "Addresses Delivered at the Colony Club," April 28, 1924.

the "competence in a chosen field" would not be guided by narrow research standards, but rather, "The field of major interest in practically every case will be broader than any single department. It may be organized around a present interest leading to a future adult activity." [40]

In the Junior Division, as has been seen above, the plan was to gain unity of subject matter by building a pattern of introductory courses around a cultural epoch. Thus, though the girl's course for the four years was geared toward performance in one line, it seems to have been originally planned that too much tendency toward grooving would be balanced by constant reference to the bigness of knowledge, and the broader, life-centered implications of the student's part in it.

College years. The gradual disappearance of the sub-plan to take a pattern of introductory courses in all fields has been discussed at some length in the preceding section. In the first two years, instead, the unifying center for knowledge, potentially at least, became the trial-major conference (see quotation, p. 91). In some divisions, this has not been the case; the trial-major conference has concerned only the work of the major field, work in other courses and fields being left to the teachers of those fields.

In the Senior Division, with three-fourths or more of the girl's work in her major field, breadth or unity of knowledge became almost wholly defined by the individual case. Administratively, the desires of the early *Plan* had been carried out by setting up academic divisions, rather than departments. Yet, in the last analysis, the determining factor became the type of major-field study the student had shown herself best fitted to do. In some cases, this might involve work of considerable scope and perspective; in others, the lion's share of her time and energies might be directed to the analysis of a couple of test tubes. "Unification of knowledge," in other words, has shown itself to be a difficult thing to project, blanket-fashion, upon a program of individually defined study within one subject-field.

[40] *The Educational Plan for Bennington College,* p. 11.

(2) "Activities" and the curriculum.

Preparatory years. Like the early plan for Sarah Lawrence, the Bennington plan from the first contemplated closing the gap between intra- and extra-class activity. Like the other college plan also, it involved direct faculty participation. Here the similarity ended. The Bennington plan, in brief, was to make the teacher responsible, not only for seeing to his student's curricular needs, but for helping her to swing her campus activities into the main stream of her educational development. The following paragraph from the *Plan* shows the unusual degree to which teacher-intervention in, indeed sponsorship of, the students' campus life was proposed, though just how the machinery of this would work is not made clear:

Here, perhaps, even more than in the case of curriculum and method, is a unique opportunity for a new college. Bennington intends to take full advantage of it. By recognizing the value of many student enterprises, by basing students' tasks upon their fundamental ambitions and interests, by setting up skill and understanding in a major field as a principal aim to which both curricular and extra-curricular activity will contribute, the college will do much toward destroying the gulf now existing between student and faculty purposes. The athletic, dramatic, musical, publication, self-government, and religious enterprises of undergraduate life, by intelligent guidance at the outset, can be incorporated into the main intellectual and artistic program sponsored by the faculty. Trivial and merely imitative student organizations will probably be proposed; but if these do not fall of their own weight they can be effectively discouraged before they become fatally imbedded in institutional tradition.[41]

College years. How the foregoing ideas fared in the actual experience of the college is difficult for the outsider to judge (and does not come within this study's main focus). Evidence of an unusual amount of faculty-student collaboration in campus activity is not especially great. Inclusion of a certain kind of recreational activities within regular "academic" work—namely, that in the fine arts and literature—on the other hand, has from the start of the college been pronounced. Part of this

[41] *Educational Plan for Bennington College*, p. 13.

may be due to the strong divisions in these fields at the college, and part, surely, to the fact that most of the instructors of literature, art, dance, drama, and music in Bennington teach from the belief that practice, theory, recreation, and "education" in these arts cannot and should not be divided from each other (see also Chap. VII). As a result, these fields have been heavily patronized. Over a third of the student body, for instance, sometime in its college course takes work in the dance. Many use it by preference to get the physical exercise which the Health Service advises.[42]

(3) Attitude toward vocational preparation.

Preparatory years. One of the centers of modern educational controversy which President Leigh did not attempt to dodge was the problem of how to reconcile the growing interest in vocational knowledge with the liberal arts. His early writings about the college show that he believed Bennington, as a college aiming toward a life-centered curriculum wherein theory and practice would merge, would find itself in a prime position to show the falsity of any such distinctions. The *Plan* states:

> Especially where a vocation has not as yet developed academic preparation beyond the undergraduate college Bennington will not hesitate to include training in the necessary minor techniques required for successful entrance to it. . . . The type of intellectual asceticism which fears that contact with practice or reality will destroy the field for culture will be studiously avoided at Bennington.[43]

It is interesting to note here, however, that the only example given of a vocation which might be thus treated was "stenography and typing."

College years. The foregoing open-arms attitude toward the vocations has been retained in the college announcements up

---

[42] On the subject of physical exercise, the college typically has put individual choice or need above general prescription. Sports and games are provided but not levied. Participation in all activities is on a voluntary basis, and is student-organized, except for professional instruction, called in seasonally from the outside. A full-time "Director of Sports" was appointed at the time of the college opening, but this office was given up after one year. Physical exercise is now checked by the Health Director.

[43] *Op. cit.*, p. 11.

through the present. The current catalog states, "There is no hesitation in relating Senior Division requirements to vocations growing out of work in the field." [44] This is later modified to the extent of: "On the other hand, vocational training is never permitted to interfere with the fundamental purpose of the Senior Division." [45]

Investigation has not discovered any group of methods at the college (excepting the Field Periods) which have worked specifically to achieve vocation-centered ends, outside the usual pre-professional work which all colleges are bound to take on. [46] Exception exists in the case of the fine arts, where the activities performed are themselves direct preparation for an after-college career. (Only a small minority of graduates each year, however, go on professionally in these fields.) The general impression is gained, omitting the special case of the fine arts, that although a vocational turn to some student's work, on her own initiative, would be thought quite acceptable, the orientation of the teaching divisions themselves toward the content of education remains pre-eminently in the customary liberal arts. (This impression, however, has not been systematically checked.) If this is a true insight, it may be due to a feeling at the college that vocational interests, after all, receive their due emphasis during the interim called the Winter Field Period.

(4) The Winter Field Period.

Preparatory years. Two natural facts about the prospective new college interfered with the picture of a place where "life-centered" learning could go on. First, it was to be a women's college. [47] Second, it was to be fairly far from any large city.

[44] *Bennington College,* "Announcement for the Year 1941–1942," p. 18.

[45] *Ibid.*

[46] In the third year of the college, an interdivisional "Human Development Major" was started, with the intention of providing extensive field-work in connection with the College Nursery School. This experiment was concluded after three years.

[47] H. C. Herring, "Education at Bennington," *Harpers,* Vol. 8, pp. 408–417, September, 1940. In this article Mr. Herring states that one of President Leigh's definite hopes was that the Bennington of the present should be only the first unit of an eventual men-and-women's college. In this connection, it is interesting to note that the Vermont charter permits giving the degree either to men or to women.

In recognition of the second obstacle, President Leigh planned to give full credit for long periods of non-resident work during the latter two years, when the individual need indicated it (such as at large university laboratories, city art centers, government bureaus, etc.). For the benefit of all, moreover, the college calendar was readjusted to this end:

In addition to a two-months' summer vacation there will be a winter recess extending from Christmas through Washington's Birthday. For both faculty and students this provision gives an opportunity for travel, for non-resident field work in groups, and for participation in metropolitan life at its most active period.[48]

College years. By and large, the number of students who have taken advantage of extended non-resident study during the college year has been small (discounting a good deal of short-term field work, such as the Bennington Survey, described below). In contrast, the winter recess, originally announced modestly as a rather minor part of the program, has been more formally organized, and has risen to become one of the most widely noticed features of the college program. The vocational side has been stressed. The plan is now described:

The winter period is designed, in general, to give students an opportunity for independent work on programs that can be better carried out away from the College. . . . These programs may consist of reading and writing, of experience in an occupation, of study at other institutions, of observation or investigation. A written report is made to the counselor, and this becomes an essential part of the student's record. . . .[49]

Among the sample areas for winter field activities noted by one instructor [50] are hospitals and clinics; a textile factory; a publishing firm, advertising department; stock companies and little theatres; dressmaking establishments; a public health department; and so on. Commenting on the educational value of the field period activity the same writer says:

[48] *The Educational Plan for Bennington College,* p. 12.
[49] *Bennington College,* "Announcement for the Year 1941–1942," p. 20.
[50] C. H. Gray, "Recess for Work Experience," *Occupations,* Vol. 14, pp. 5–9, October, 1935.

The important problem is to use the vocational aim as a stimulus to and focus for education in a broad field of human knowledge or activity, the value of which does not lie solely in its usefulness as an avenue to a bread-winning job, but mainly in the cultivation of the student's understanding of her field in relation to the rest of human life.[51]

c. Methods for socializing individual education.

Preparatory years. The movement for Bennington College was born in the individualistic twenties, when out-and-out cultural and economic laissez-faire, on a national scale, was having its last fling. It would be unreasonable to expect that the *Educational Plan* for the college, written in the late years of this epoch, should have shown any outspoken conflicts with the spirit of the times. Reading the *Plan* brings no large impressions of anything which might compromise the individual-centered base of the program; nor do any of the eighteen listed "essential features of the Bennington Program" directly concern working toward the large-scale social aim. Exception might be claimed for the idea to orient the first two years toward an understanding of Western culture, and for the housing plans, which included the intention: "Bennington will derive its varied student body from the operation of the selective scholarship plan, while its community life and atmosphere will lead to utilizing this variety for the stimulating exchange of ideas and attitudes based upon real tolerance and understanding." [52]

College years. The first catalog ended its list of ten aims with one which stressed (see above, p. 80), "social responsibility, social participation and cooperation rather than aloofness." For the long-range and short-range carrying-out of this aim, both of the plans just mentioned ran into some fairly inevitable compromises. The crowding-out of the Western-culture idea for the introductory courses by a preoccupation with the major study has already been referred to. And in the case of the housing arrangements, the selective scholarship plan (though it now

[51] *Ibid.,* p. 6.
[52] *The Educational Plan for Bennington College,* p. 14.

affects, in some degree, some two-fifths of the students) has not yet greatly lessened the large majority of girls from comfort-able-to-wealthy homes.

To some extent social education at the college is made pos-sible by the fact that the Bennington community functions as a social unit, in which an unusual amount of responsibility is made the official business of the student body. To quote from the current catalog:

The organized life of the College, especially of the student houses, serves inevitably as a laboratory for education in problems of social control, individual liberty, group deliberation and cooperation, choice and support of group leaders.[53]

To what degree such social autonomy works successfully is not within the business of this discussion. Aside from the lim-iting fact that such a selective community cannot hope really to reproduce the outside social scene, chances for training in these areas would seem to be good.

A social orientation for the student's academic work itself, beyond the matter of the individual teacher's influence (as on all campuses), is somewhat hampered by the physical remote-ness of the college. This can perhaps be made up for to con-siderable degree by the Winter Field Period. There is no rea-son, on the other hand, to believe that just moving during that period from a laboratory in Bennington to one in, say, Colum-bia will do anything for the social education of that particular student. The winter project, in other words, would have to be one which *definitely plans* for the type of "larger-centered" so-cial experience desired.

Meanwhile, the most important evidence toward society-cen-tered education at Bennington is furnished by the "Benning-ton Survey," in which social studies students have engaged since 1933. This yearly project is described by one of its in-vestigators:

The Bennington Survey was designed in the second year of the college to broaden the educational experience of students of the so-

[53] Bennington College, *op. cit.,* p. 23.

cial sciences through training in the actual gathering, refining, and analyzing of raw data. The Survey is continuous and cumulative, and consists of related student projects dealing with various aspects of society, past and present, in Bennington, Vermont.[54]

Although there might be some doubt whether the conservative New England community likes the idea of being put under the college student's lens, the testimony is reassuring:

Civic organizations have made use of student findings. That is to say, Town and Gown relations, historically marked by frontier incidents and violent reprisals, have been improved by student investigations in neighboring communities.[55]

The educational trend of such activities, aside from the limiting fact that they touch only students of one division, sounds in keeping with current social-centered emphases in college education. This may be particularly true if the "Survey" activities described move beyond the stage of mutual inspection to *joint efforts on the part of town and gown* toward cooperative regional work. There is some evidence, for example in the college's participation in community chest work, that such efforts are becoming more frequently tried. As is true in most college communities, the war situation has brought a decided growth of college-and-community solidarity and action.

Despite all such positive signs, however, the situation of a college given to a free system of individualized education, suddenly set down in the midst of a quiet, native-New England countryside, has created only one of several inescapable problems of social adjustment and education which the college must work continually towards solving.

Evaluation and control.

Preparatory and college years. One of the semi-popular lay fancies about Bennington has been of the college country club where girls come to be catered to, or to park their belongings while they week-end in even palmier regions elsewhere. More

[54] T. P. Brockway, "The Community in a Social Studies Program: The Bennington Survey," *Middle States Association of History and Social Science Teachers; Proceedings*, p. 62, 1939.
[55] *Ibid.*

seriously, some amount of outside opinion has been gained that there is no systematic checking or correction of what they do during their college course.

Such illusions may have come from an original misinterpretation of President Leigh's *Educational Plan,* leading to the belief that neither examinations nor failures would find place at the college. Such was not the original intention. It is true that the *Plan* said (p. 6): "No mere satisfaction of rules of class attendance, reading of specified books, or accumulation of course credits will suffice." But the real dynamics of the Bennington plans for evaluation sprang from the next sentence (already quoted above), "Your degree will be given on the basis of a demonstration that you have learned how to stand on your own feet and to work with skill and understanding *in your chosen field.*" [56] This was borne out in the standards later established for decision on promotion to the Senior Division: "(1) demonstrated ability to do advanced work in the proposed major field and (2) sustained interest in the field as manifested by a capacity for independent activity." [57] An evaluation system based upon a one-study criterion like this could therefore permit such an unconventionality as: "Failure to do satisfactory work in one or more courses outside of the field of the student's choice will not disqualify or delay her," [58] without departing from the rigor of its plan.

It is interesting to note, furthermore, that evaluation in the one thing that was to count, i.e., the major field, was originally rather formally planned:

> The Bennington degree will be awarded as the result of examinations, theses or other tests designed to reveal objectively the accomplishment of the student in her field of major study.[59]

What happened to such formal plans may recall the case of Sarah Lawrence. Here too, it was found that a system which had committed itself to educating the student in terms of her

[56] *Ibid.* Italics mine.
[57] *Bennington College,* "Announcement for the Third Year, 1934–1935," p. 15.
[58] *The Educational Plan,* p. 10.
[59] *Ibid.,* p. 13.

individual case did not readily allow the kind of comparability which would make tests and grading workable. The concentrated work of the student in one field typically led to a unique product which had to be judged on its own merits. Accordingly, in the College Catalog for the third year, the statement was changed to read that the degree would be awarded "as a result of such tests, reports, and other specific accomplishments as the Division sets up." [60] In practice, formal examinations in the college, especially in the Senior Division, have been rare.

Meanwhile, evaluation at the other stages of the student's career likewise for the most part came to be qualitatively arranged.[61] With the predominance of the individual conference as a teaching method, evaluation devices, including papers, reports, "quizzes," et al., can be made to fall into their natural place in the teaching process. At the same time, it permits the instructor to accumulate a good deal of evidence of many kinds for appraising the student, which in turn is submitted to the proper central bodies when the time arrives for deciding on promotion to the Senior Division, or on the awarding of the A.B.

The official system of evaluation which has resulted at Bennington proceeds, in summary, as follows:

Twice a year, or when work is dropped or finished, each instructor sends the girl's counselor a report of her work with him. This report lists judgments on subject-matter covered; aims pointed toward; teaching methods used; written and oral work done; an accomplishment rating; and supplementary information about the student that will be helpful to the counselor, including any material to be used confidentially.

From these records, added to his own, the counselor makes his summary. The December report is shown to the girl. The June report comes to her in the form of a letter from the president.

The counselor's records come partly from monthly sheets submitted by the student, listing all work covered. He and she also

[60] *Bennington College, op. cit.,* p. 20. Some sort of Senior Project has become the usual chief evidence for graduation.

[61] This excludes the American Council on Education standard objective examinations on General Culture, English, Science, etc., which, for diagnostic purposes, are regularly used.

make out, in season, a Winter and Summer Field Period report, giving work plans, work done, and counselor's evaluation.

Minutes are kept of the action of the Committee on Student Personnel on the girl's promotion to Senior Division. At this meeting the faculty of her major division are present. The minutes are filed in her folder in the Personnel Office.

In concluding the discussion of the evaluation question at Bennington, it may be asked wherein does the college, in evaluating, officially recognize its commitments to educate "the whole personality of the student." Answer to this may be implicit in the comment, "Counselling is the heart of Bennington's scheme." [62] As the girl's combined counsellor-and-major-subject tutor, the adviser has been in a position to bring together, for his own and others' benefits, a good deal of evidence of all types about his advisee. (All kinds of data about the student, except her medical record, are kept in cumulative file, to which he has easy access.) It is nevertheless true that, perhaps because of the major-study base to the adviser-student relationship, counseling at the college has tended to flow chiefly through the channel of the girl's educational, rather than personal, experiences and problems. The manifest feeling at Bennington, to date, is probably correctly expressed: "The wise counselor abjures the role of confessor and sticks to the role of friendly instructor." [63] Whether this attitude is in all cases applicable and at all times "wise," it is not the business here to consider.

Admissions policies.

Throughout the discussion up to now it has been hard to separate the other topics reviewed from one fundamentally important element of the college, namely, the kind of girl who was to be encouraged to come. The applicant's record was, and officially still is, to be characterized in two main respects.

Preparatory and college years. Dr. Kilpatrick in his Colony Club address of 1924 had given as his first working aim for a

[62] Herring, *op. cit.,* p. 413.
[63] *Ibid.*

new college program, "A new deal on college entrance requirements, to free secondary education from the bondage to
colleges." [64] This, at that time, was a thing sorely needed.[65]
The typical high or preparatory school offered for the bulk of
its students an ancient formula including Latin, much mathematics, foreign languages, etc. When asked why they clung to
this schedule, refusing to change such studies or add newer
ones, they answered, rightly, that the colleges required this
preparation. Although the new, progressive schools rebelled
against this evidence of the academic lock-step, their cause was
likewise shackled by their obligation, after all, to get their students accepted into college.

A first point made by the admissions policy for Bennington
College, then, aimed generally at helping the cause of the new
secondary schools, by specifically announcing:

> The requirements are not stated in terms of a standard group of
> fifteen units in which students may be certified or pass examinations.
> *The content and methods of work in the schools are left to the
> schools themselves,* where they properly belong in this period of
> fruitful educational construction.[66]

The minimum, *and* maximum, of the applicant's record, on
the quantitative side, was thus stated to be *successful completion of the secondary school course.*

On the positive side a stipulation was made which has perhaps done more than any single thing to establish the particular character of Bennington College up to 1942. This stipulation, from 1928 until last year, was not essentially changed:

> The object of the Bennington admissions system is to discover and
> to select girls of serious interest and of unusual promise in one or
> more of the four major fields into which serious human achieve-
> ment is . . . divided. . . .[67]

How "serious" an interest in one field a girl must show evidence of having before being judged worthy of admission has

[64] "Addresses Delivered at the Colony Club," April 28, 1924.
[65] See Aiken, *The Story of the Eight Year Study,* 1942.
[66] *The Educational Plan for Bennington College,* p. 7. Italics mine.
[67] *Ibid.,* p. 6.

provided something of a perennial problem to the admissions officers. That the president himself recognized this problem is borne out in the addition, ". . . at Bennington, as elsewhere, students with uniformly good records will be welcomed," [68] and, later, in the prediction, "Others will come to college with temporary enthusiasms, preferences and aversions. . . . Still others, although of good intellectual ability, will as yet have developed no well-defined purposes . . . or . . . interests." [69] On the whole, in practice the "special interest" criterion has had to be rather freely interpreted, and tempered by a good measure of insight about the applicant's other, and possibly more reliable, traits.

Notwithstanding, as a commitment maintained by the college, it has served in no uncertain manner both to influence the nature of the student body [70] and to promote the individualized, major-study program of the college during its first ten years.

CONCLUSION

In the much-quoted *Educational Plan for Bennington College,* President Leigh noted (p. 9) that "The Bennington curriculum, admissions system, and scholarship system depend organically upon each other." From this chapter's analysis, it now seems correct to add to that organic relationship the aims of the college, the teaching methods, and the evaluation system;—in short, the "organism" becomes the total Bennington educational program. The nature of that organism has been shown to be, first, a system which attempted to build its content and method differently for each different student; and, second, one which placed competence in one subject-field as the

[68] *Ibid.,* p. 7.

[69] *Ibid.,* p. 9.

[70] There has been some discussion outside as to whether an admissions policy of this kind tended to attract the freakish. About this Dr. Leigh had to say, in *Progressive Education,* September, 1932 ("Bennington Gets Under Way," p. 372), "Although girls of specialized excellence can gain admission to Bennington, in preference to those with uniform but mediocre records, it is interesting to note that most of the girls already admitted are of the versatile rather than the specialized types."

main goal of her educational task.[71] The experience of the college in meeting both these working aims at once has, typically, produced a different working solution for each case. Some important elements in that solution which have been seen to vary accordingly are the size and intensity of the student's major-study; its main point of reference—i.e., academic, vocational, social, or other—; her acquaintance with outside fields; and the degree of her capitalization of the general life and activities of the college. Through it all, the college has sought to live up to a primary commitment as [72] "a place not where courses are offered but where individuals are educated." This commitment, whatever the changes that have recently been made (see pp. 141–144), may probably be expected to continue.

[71] The college yearly in its announcement sponsors also "the promotion of health, desirable habits and attitudes, breadth of knowledge and a variety of amateur interests, emotional maturity and stable character, individual and social responsibility . . . ," but, more wisely than some colleges, adds, "They are not measurable by the award of the degree; they are not all directly attainable by students and it is not practically possible to set up for them a minimum of attainment."

[72] W. Fowlie, "The Bennington Experiment," *The French Review*, p. 101, December, 1937.

Chapter V

The Bard Program

IF BENNINGTON COLLEGE came on to the college scene as a kind of newborn organism, Bard, a residential college of Columbia University, has arrived at its present form by what might rather fancily be called "a process of successive regeneration." It is true that the program which forms the base of operations at present was evolved, as was Bennington, in one comprehensive document. Yet as a result of different administrations both before and after the proposal of its modern program, the college has seen some four stages in the realizing of its educational plan.

Bard, in a word, is one of the examples of those institutions mentioned in Chapter I which choose to go through the pain and hard work of fitting a new college into the framework of the old. The process has been featured by all the difficulties usually associated with it, plus financial hardships far more acute than those which the other two colleges in this study have had to face. That it has come through its trials with a program and spirit closely comparable to theirs seems an educational feat worthy of notice and admiration. The focus of this study, however, commits it to looking dispassionately at the college record, not as a story of administrative labors, but as a series of developments in the content and method of its program.

HISTORICAL SUMMARY

Geographically speaking, Bard is not widely known. In the educator's world, it is not nearly so well known as the relative uniqueness of its program would lead one to guess.[1] In contrast to the tremendous attention and interest paid the founding and development of Bennington, this, on the outside, seems surprising. Part of an answer may lie in the probability that the sponsorship of Bennington by wide numbers of laymen and educators was a happy accident of time and circumstance for which few colleges can reasonably dare hope. Part also may lie in the fact that Bard has not in the past happened to have a head so inclined toward legitimate educational publicity as was President Leigh of Bennington. A good deal of the rest, however, may be attributed to the gradual, rather than dramatic, emergence of the Bard College plan for Individual Education,[2] through the stages of four different administrations (not including two Acting Deans) within eight years.

The precursor of Bard, St. Stephen's College, was founded in 1860 by John Bard, with the assistance of a group of lay and clerical members of the Episcopal Church.[3] The college was, and still is, located on a portion of John Bard's estate in Annandale-on-Hudson, Dutchess County, New York. During all but the last of its seventy-five years under its original name, the college functioned, on an enrollment varying between eighteen and one hundred forty students, as a denominational college for men offering a traditional program of classical and scientific studies toward the A.B. degree.

In 1928 Dr. B. I. Bell, Warden of St. Stephen's, and President Butler of Columbia effected an agreement by which St. Stephen's joined the growing federation of colleges under Columbia University. An interlocking membership was established between the two Boards of Trustees. St. Stephen's retained its own budget and financial holdings; but in the next

[1] Twenty-six out of 60 Eastern secondary school heads, when asked by letter to return certain solicited opinions about the Bard program, added the unsolicited comment that their opinions were hampered by lack of adequate knowledge about the college. R. D. Leigh, "Final Report to the President and Trustees of Bard College" (mimeographed), p. 98. 1940.

[2] This term was used as the title for the *Bulletin of Bard College*, Vol. 80, March, 1940.

[3] Historical data from college bulletins and, chiefly, pages 134–148 of Dr. Leigh's 1940 "Report," in which he presents a condensation of variously gathered historical data about St. Stephen's and Bard.

few years, thanks partly to the depression, funds were borrowed
from Columbia to help maintain the college. In 1933 Dr. Bell
gave up the Wardenship, and the University took a more active
hand in affairs, eventually appointing Dr. Donald G. Tewksbury of Teachers College to be Acting Dean (he became Dean
the following year).

After a year of study on the problem, Dean Tewksbury came
forth with a comprehensive proposal for an entirely new college program. This plan (known locally as "the Blue Document") proposed "reorganizing the institution with the purpose of making a thoroughly modern college program fully in
line with prevailing thought and practice regarding educational reform." [4] With the aid of a grant of $10,000 from the
Carnegie Corporation, further financial help from Columbia,
and an increased tuition, the new plan was put into effect. The
college was gradually secularized; the name, on Dean Tewksbury's suggestion, was officially changed by the trustees in
March, 1935, to Bard College; and, in line with the need to
bring best available energies to bear upon putting across the
new program, a considerable turnover of faculty was humanely
but forthrightly made.[5] New teachers who gave promise of doing a good job under the features of the modern plan were
brought in.

Owing partly to the fact that the trustee board was not so
quickly changed to harmonize with the change, financial difficulties persisted, and eventually led Dr. Tewksbury to resign,
in 1937. There followed a period of uncertainty, during which
Dean Herbert Hawkes of Columbia served, in absentia, as Acting Dean. In 1938 Dr. Harold Mestre of the Biology Department, who had functioned during the year in the temporary
office of Director of Studies, was appointed Dean. In September, 1939, in the opening week of college, he suddenly died.

---

[4] Leigh, *op. cit.,* p. 144.

[5] See Committee on Academic Freedom and Tenure, *Association of American
University Professors Bulletin,* Vol. 21, p. 595, December, 1935. This committee
reports "no question of legality" in the dismissal of Bard teachers, and noted,
"care has been taken to make financial adjustments with all the teachers who
were dropped." All in all, the investigation found nothing to criticize.

During the ensuing interim President Leigh of Bennington, since the college's beginning a close and sympathetic observer, temporarily left Bennington to become Acting Dean of Bard. Following his semester's study of the college and its needs, the Trustees of the college appointed the present Dean, Charles Harold Gray, then of the Bennington Literature Division, in January, 1940.[6]

During Dean Gray's two and a half years in office, the enrollment of the college has grown to its highest sustained figure, around one hundred forty; buildings and equipment have been renovated and improved; a new school of research, the Institute for Economic Education, has been added; and these and other changes have in general placed the college on perhaps the best footing in its history.

Primary college aims.

It is well-nigh impossible to put a new college into the setting of an old and not inherit some influence from the bygone school. The very walls of the old seem to give out an air which impregnates even the most modern, radically different successor. In the case of St. Stephen's and Bard, a more tangible factor than environmental atmosphere has kept a thread of continuity between the two: one that is certainly not to the latter's disadvantage nor the former's discredit. This is the factor of the small, intimate undergraduate college.

True, the original objective as stated in the founding of St. Stephen's gives out a note which does not sound very much like presently announced aims:

The Trustees of St. Stephen's College, for purpose of establishing, conducting, and maintaining in Red Hook, Dutchess County, a college of arts, letters, and sciences which also shall provide for the Christian training of young men who design to enter the sacred ministry in the Protestant Episcopal Church. . . .[7]

The essential nature of the college, however, was that of a small, liberal arts college with a high faculty-student ratio.

[6] Dr. Gray had served in 1935 as Acting President of Bennington College.
[7] "Amended Charter of Bard College as of July, 1939."

Putting aside for a moment the nature and content of the instruction of this traditional, classics-minded school, it is interesting to read in the old St. Stephen's statements a belief about a *method* of educating which would feel at home today in the most up-to-date progressive school: namely, the attention to be given by the teacher to the individual learner. Whether it be Socrates and Plato, Mark Hopkins on the log, or a classics-bound college, this intimate relationship between teacher and pupil lasts through the years as a chief point of support for the small school.

A sample of various official statements may show how St. Stephen's hewed to this line.

In his opening address to the students, Reverend R. B. Fairbairn, Warden of the college from 1863 to 1898, said:

> Will a class of twenty under a Professor of Latin not learn more Latin than a class of forty or one hundred? . . . when you sit down in a classroom to learn Latin or Geometry, or the elements of logic in order that the powers of your mind may be called into operation, you may be glad that there are not more than twenty associated with you, in order that the drill may be carried on day after day to your individual advantage.[8]

Some fifty years later, Warden Bell, in the college announcement, carried on essentially the same beliefs:

> The College is small. It has neither the desire nor the intention ever of enrolling over two hundred and fifty students. It wishes to be judged from a qualitative rather than a quantitative standard. . . . Its methods of teaching are direct and personal, in accord with the best pedagogical thought of today.[9]

The catalog, up to the year the change to Bard was made, also carried the statement:

> Because of the intimacy of the college, it is possible for the authorities to make the individual acquaintance of every man and to feel for him a real interest.[10]

This individual-oriented aim, at least, provides the thread

---

[8] R. B. Fairbairn, *Intellectual Education in Small Colleges*, p. 59. 1880.
[9] *Catalogue of St. Stephen's College, 1933–1934*, p. 10.
[10] *Ibid.*

between the old college and the present program. Examination of the "Blue Document" [11] shows they came, in their modern context, to occupy the heart of the aims for the Bard College that was to be.

Appearing first in Dean Tewksbury's 1934 document, and thereafter in unchanged form in the college catalogs up until Dean Gray's administration (1940), those aims were stated to be:

(1) The student's approach to his college work should be made through the individual abilities, interests, and purposes which he has discovered during the years of his previous educational experience;

(2) these motivating elements in the life of the individual should be the center around which he should proceed to build his curriculum; and

(3) his college education following the lines of expanding interest and changing purpose should culminate in a broad cultural outlook.[12]

Aim number one established the connection between the small college of the past, which also featured its own brand of individual attention and the modern college, which was trying to build a scientifically "right" education for each student on the individuating principle.

Such a connection is often claimed by apologists for the small, traditional college to show that the new college has nothing that the old college had not, but is merely inventing fancy terms for the same thing. These arguments pull a cloth over the underlying broad gap between. Admitting the fact that the old college gave its students individual attention in learning their intellectual tasks, it remained true that *the nature of those tasks,* and the results expected from them, *were almost entirely defined in terms of subject matter and tradition, and could as a matter of fact be as far as the moon from the actual nature and needs of the boy who was performing them.*

[11] D. G. Tewksbury, "An Educational Program for St. Stephen's College"; A Preliminary Statement Submitted for the Consideration of the Board of Trustees of the College. 1934.

[12] *Ibid.,* p. 3.

In the meantime, the cue to the basic difference is given by aim number two, "these motivating elements in the life of the individual should be the center around which he should proceed to build his own curriculum. . . ." Here we see the logical continuity, implied in the foregoing analyses of Sarah Lawrence and Bennington, between truly fitting the education around the individual and, *ipso facto,* making the core of that education vital (life-like) to him. It is true that in the actual choice of subject matter for study which follows, there is a good deal of latitude possible in deciding what, after all, *is* "life-like" for each student. It may be decided that a certain course in French Romanticism is or can be "life-like" to him; or it may be decided that life-like study can only become a fact by the student's going out and observing some section of actual ongoing life: a county farm, or a steel mill. Or a course involving some of both types of experience may be arranged. The location of the eventual methods at Bard, along this line between book-learning and life-learning, is a matter for the discussion of the course and methods of study below.

The plan for the Bard program was not meant to end with the fitting of each educational pattern around each boy and the building of a life-like course of study by means of this process. The ultimate direction of the pattern was turned outward toward the acquiring of "a broad cultural outlook." Although this has the sound of a society-centered aim, it is not clear from its phrasing alone just how far this was intended to mean a *concern for,* as well as an enlightened understanding of, the problems and progress of society. That the college should properly move beyond the area of polite acquaintance with social problems, however, into the area of moving the student to want to do something about them is made more specifically clear in a later section of the original proposal:

The college may assist him to learn, in the midst of the community of which he is a member, the art of living harmoniously and helpfully with his fellow men. It may encourage him to develop an increasing sense of responsibility, as he meets the demands of life within and without the college. It may exert an influence to lead him to a clear appreciation and understanding of the moral hazards, problems, and tasks which occupy so large a part of the life of a man. We betray youth if we fail in these things.[13]

To summarize the review of the original Bard's "underlying principles of the new program," the three points have been seen to come rather remarkably close to the main aims discovered for the other two colleges in this study. Although the evolved methods discussed below may show reasonable differences in Bard's way of meeting the aims, this closeness is so marked that there seems no difficulty in using for the further study of this college, also, the triple classification of aims and methods: (1) those for individual study; (2) those for vitalizing learning; and (3) those for socializing individual education.

That Dean Gray's administration at Bard, from 1940 to the present, has accepted the above aims might be thought probable at the outset because of the fact that Dr. Gray came from Bennington, where he had been an active proponent of the original program.[14] (The superposition of this background upon the Tewksbury-Bard structure has made an interesting synthesis which will be discussed in the next section.) The aims are now stated in the catalog to read:

The most legitimate claim for a good college education is that it can pry a student's eyes part way open to what is going on in his world and can help him to see what he can do to take his part in it. . . . His years in college, whatever else they do, must set going his own conscious efforts towards self-education. The studies he engages in and all the procedures and methods of the college should be chosen with this primary aim in view.[15]

The foregoing statement (displaying a down-to-earth modesty rather rare in college statements) thus seems to combine the aims of individual and vital education into an appeal to that quality which has been seen to underlie much of the progressive college doctrine—namely, "self-education." In another statement the component elements are more clearly seen:

[13] *Ibid.*, p. 24.

[14] During Dean Mestre's brief period as Dean there was no change in the official statement of college aims.

[15] *Bulletin of Bard College, 1942–1943*, p. 3.

The first thing we try for is to catch the young man's curiosity and keep it alive as the driving force in all his education. . . . In order to approach this . . . we find it necessary to work individually with our students. As we work individually with our students we come closely into contact with their personalities. We are interested in their growth in all respects.[16]

A continuity between the present administration's statements of college aims and two of the three of the original Bard program is thus found. That a specific mention of social aims, also, is not found may be due more than anything else to the limited amount of available statements, as yet, about the contemporary program. A more accurate check, however, should be the study of actual operations going on in the college at the present time.

In the discussion of underlying college aims, finally, the question may be asked, has Bard, along with Sarah Lawrence and Bennington, openly declared itself inspired by the progressive movement in education? The answer seems to depend more on inference than direct discovery. That it has been assumed by those who have observed the college is indicated by a matter-of-fact reference in *School and Society* magazine to, "Bard College, the only college for boys in the East that avowedly adheres to the tenets of the Progressive School of educational theory. . . ." [17]

In the original "Blue Document," no such out-and-out reference is found. On personal advice from Dr. Tewksbury it is known, as a matter of fact, that he drew inspiration, especially for his four-year major-study plan, from the best he saw in the great English universities. It may be that this attitude influenced him to prefer, for reasons of his own, not to consign his program to the authority of the progressive movement in this country.

Nevertheless, the statement on the first page of Tewksbury's

[16] C. H. Gray, "First Report to the President of Columbia University and the Board of Trustees, Bard College," *School and Society*, Vol. 52, p. 456, November 9, 1940.

[17] "The New Four-Year Plan at Bard College," *School and Society*, Vol. 52, p. 456, November 9, 1940.

original proposal hardly leaves any doubt that he saw his college carrying on those same new educational trends which the early statements of Sarah Lawrence and Bennington openly attributed to the tenets of the progressive schools of the day:

> There is an insistent demand on the part of educators, parents, and young men alike that our colleges and universities provide among other things for a greater flexibility in the academic curriculum, for more adequate attention to individual needs and abilities, for larger recognition of the arts in the instructional program, for a more realistic approach to the problems of contemporary life, and withal for an increasing emphasis on quality and distinction in the educational program.[18]

The program which came out in 1934 carried enough features like those of Bennington, while showing at the same time an individuality of its own, to prompt educational observers to label them sister-colleges.[19] That this may indicate for each a lineage stretching back to the English tutorial and majors plan seems probable, though it is something which must be left to specific investigation elsewhere. In the meantime, the evidence here has shown that Bard's original author designed the program to aim precisely in the direction aimed by the other two colleges in this study. Such a fact seems more important to this discussion than the question of why it was not chosen, at that time, officially to place the label "progressive" upon the college.[20] That the identity was further established by the emerging methods themselves should come to light in the following discussion.

---

[18] Tewksbury, *op. cit.*, p. 1.

[19] In an editorial, "Experiment in educational methods to be tried by Bard College," *New Republic,* Vol. 81, p. 234, January 9, 1935, the program was observed to be "following somewhat the path marked out for the women students of Bennington College."

D. P. Cottrell, in his chapter "General Education in Experimental Liberal Arts Colleges," in *General Education in the American College,* frequently finds reason to speak of the programs of Bennington and Bard in conjunction. See especially pp. 210–211.

[20] It is probably significant that Dr. Tewksbury taught at Sarah Lawrence before going to St. Stephen's as Dean. During his Deanship before and after the change to Bard, conferences between President Leigh of Bennington and himself were held.

The course and method of study.

The first concrete design for Sarah Lawrence was made in 1926; the first Bennington plan, after five years of preparations, was issued late in 1928. In some contrast, the Bard program is only eight years old. Its fairly short career should enable the discussion to treat the development in each area of methods somewhat in one continuous piece.

a. Methods of individual study.

The core of the student's academic experience, in the original Bard plan, was to be his progress through a major-field of his choice during most or all of his four years. This, to Dean Tewksbury, was the logical educational equivalent of the aim (see above) ". . . motivating elements in the life of the individual should be the center around which he should . . . build his own curriculum. . . ." Accordingly, the entering student was to be advised that "after ample time and opportunity is given for consultation with members of the faculty during the opening weeks of the college, he will be asked to decide for himself in what field he will try his powers." [21] The supporting belief for this early step was added in that first plan,

In general, the earlier he makes the right decision and the more steadily he follows the line which he has chosen the more vigorous and substantial will be his growth.[22]

In another statement, an interesting correspondingly negative opinion was also given:

This procedure will avoid the danger run by other colleges which postpone selection of a field of concentration until the beginning of the sophomore or the junior year—the danger of the weakening or loss of those initial enthusiasms and vital interests which the individual brings to college.[23]

The major-study at Bard, furthermore, was not planned as a

[21] Tewksbury, *op. cit.,* p. 7.

[22] *Ibid.,* p. 8.

[23] D. G. Tewksbury, "The Educational Program of Bard College," *School and Home,* Vol. 16, p. 651, April, 1935.

"trial-major" (this term came into the college after Tewksbury's administration; see below). Although it was expected that the student would continue to explore in other fields for the purpose of confirming himself in his choice of a field or finding the need to change, continuity, not change, was the virtue emphasized. For a chief purpose that its author held for it, the major-study plan was projected to serve as a steady focal point throughout the student's four years.

A review of that educational purpose may perhaps help to clarify Tewksbury's reasons for the four-year major plan.

In his Blue Document, the new dean had offered as a premise,

> It is generally recognized that a truly liberal education must have two constituents: the development of insight and penetration into a particular field, in which an individual's powers may approach the ideals of mastery; and the attainment of breadth of outlook and understanding in the field of human culture as a whole. *It is essential that the two constituents be combined in an organic process.*[24]

The "penetration" in the plan, obviously, was to come from the four-year major. Unlike most college plans, the "breadth" was not assigned to a different area of the program; *it, also, was to be attached to the main major-study process.* To do this required, as Tewksbury intended, a different view of major field study from the usual, research-groove idea. To explain how he wished the major, and indeed the whole college course, to be pursued, he put forth an analogy which in his educational region has become mildly famous (and which will occupy a considerable place in the concluding chapter of this study):

> Such a thesis involves a reversal of the usual procedure in the planning of a college curriculum. Instead of proceeding from generalization to specialization, it is proposed that specialized experience during the early years of the college course be made the means of approach to general culture. . . . Under such a program the development of the mind of the student would be analogous to the growth of a tree which roots itself thoroughly in some particular plot of ground, develops in time a trunk of stable and living proportions,

[24] Tewksbury, *op. cit.*, pp. 3–4. Italics mine.

and finally reaches out through its branches towards the fulfillment of its life purpose. . . . such an analogy stands in contrast to the usual conception of a college curriculum as a pyramid which covers a wide area at its base and narrows to a point at its apex.[25]

The foregoing picture of an academic career holds two requirements for the college curriculum which might be called —to use words worn somewhat thin by this study—the qualitative and the quantitative. To explain the former, such an assignment for the major study as Tewksbury made consciously called for the best of "liberalizing" teaching, in a close, personalized relationship.[26] To build out from this major-study core, secondly, the nature and method of the rest of the curriculum needed to be such as to give the student some minimum mechanical aids for the "rooting," "branching out," correlating, and performing of other enriched study-activities which the plan proposed. Hence it should be interesting to review the actual methods which evolved at Bard in the first few years to carry out their working aims.

The student's program was arranged to consist essentially of four regular subject-matter courses, typically meeting as small discussion groups with an instructor. The pattern of courses that was to be taken by the student was a matter to be worked out according to his case, by himself and his adviser. It is worthy of note here, however, that in spite of the emphasis upon the major study as a main liberalizing agent, the general spread of the course program also, in the first two years, was given an horizon-expanding function which it was expected the students would more or less systematically use:

It will be expected that students will wish during the first two years to explore the other fields of culture. General introductory courses will be offered in each department of the College.[27]

[25] *Ibid.,* pp. 4–5.

[26] On personal advice, it is known that Dean Tewksbury, being asked at the outset by the faculty how much of the student's time they might devote to the major, replied that they might, if they desired, use the whole time—provided they try really to "liberalize" their students through the medium of that major-study time.

[27] D. G. Tewksbury, "An Educational Program for St. Stephen's College," p. 8. 1934.

It was also expected that in the upper years, to aid in the "branching-out" process, outside course work would continue despite the large degree of concentration on the major-study.

Concerning the all-important major-study, and the intimate connection it was to have with the student's individual development through college, it is somewhat surprising at first to find that the medium for this work centered also in a conventional taking of regularly scheduled courses. But in two aspects of the method of these courses the individuation that one might expect is found: (1) The student for the first year or two normally took two of his four courses in his chosen major field. These courses were then to be presented in a manner which might hit two birds with one stone—one bird being the majoring student, the other being a non-major taking the course for general exploratory purposes; viz.:

> The plan of such courses is to give students who wish to prepare themselves for further work (in that field) different readings and assignments from those appropriate for the general student. . . . As the needs and interests of the members of the group manifest themselves, the course may divide into smaller units or groups for the remainder of the year. . . .[28]

(2) The second device for individual treatment through regular courses came from the general expectation that, owing to small enrollment and high teacher-student ratio, the teacher should make regular use of his chance to have a tutorial conference with each student at least once a fortnight. This method was to be applied to all courses. For the major student, since two courses were in his field, it thus became possible to have weekly tutorial guidance in his own individualized course of study, through the medium of his chosen field.

The instructor primarily looked to for the task of helping the student free himself from course restraints and build his program around his developing interests was the boy's adviser.[29]

---

[28] *Bulletin of Bard College, 1934–35*, pp. 21–22.

[29] *Ibid.*, p. 15: "A general adviser assists the student in working out an integrated program of studies built around his chosen field and counsels with him on matters relating to his progress in the task of self-education."

Presumably this would be a teacher of one of the boy's two courses in his major-field. Yet under the stated program it may be noticed that this adviser officially was scheduled to see his advisee only once every two weeks, no more than any of the boy's other teachers. Whether this mere lack of official regulation sufficed to de-emphasize the relationship, or whether the press of normal teaching load hindered the individual conference schedule, in practice the close and constant collaboration between adviser and student became one of the less realized working aims of the program. Although this did not necessarily hamper individualized study, it probably took from the student's major-field study some of the enrichment and guidance that was needed to fulfill the general expectations held.

To summarize the individual-centered methods of Dean Tewksbury's Bard plan, the student's program, which centered in a progress through a chosen major field, was carried out in a pattern of regularly scheduled, subject-matter courses. Besides his major work, he was generally expected, though not required, to explore all the chief subject-fields. Both in major and in non-major study his chance to pursue learning in his own way, and to define the content of what he learned, was officially provided by *an individualized system of assigning work in his classes,* and by *the arrangement of periodic tutorial conferences for each course.*

Dr. Mestre's administration has left little available evidence of curricular change. It was a period of uncertainty in the college history, and actual progress in curriculum content and method seems to have been small. The statements of the program in the catalogs were left for the most part unchanged. One trend (possibly originating in the earlier years) which represents a small retrenchment so far as individual education is concerned was the growth in the practice of taking one introductory course in each of the four fields, from a convention into something of a blanket requirement.

The advent of Harold Gray of Bennington as Dean in 1940

brought to Bard the influence of a college program that, despite natural differences and separate origins, had been working in close parallel. This closeness is evidenced by the opinions of present members of the staff that Bard now is coming nearer to fulfilling the original aims for the college, as they interpret them, than at any period in its eight-year history. This, however, should be judged by a review of the present changes.

Following the statement of aims (as quoted above), the current catalog now has to say, relative to "generalization" or "specialization" for the beginning college student,

Bard College adopts the common sense view that the best education begins with what the student thinks is most important for him at the time and goes on from there. Instead of the uncontrolled elective system or the prescribed course for everybody regardless of tastes and abilities, the program is directed towards finding the best course of study for each individual.[80]

With this obvious agreement with the early plan, the entering student, as might be expected, thus selects a major study as before. The difference is that his choice is now called a "trial major," as at Bennington. The use of this device proceeds much as at the college where it originated (see above, Chapter IV, pp. 87ff.).

A program of four courses is still the basis of procedure. As before at Bard, the student elects two courses in his major field, the other two outside. One important change from the former system, however, gives the cue to the essential difference between the individualizing methods of the old and the new curriculums: one of these two major-field courses is now actually called "Trial Major" (as, in Art, Science, etc.). The content of this Trial-Major course then becomes defined by what teacher and student, as the year progresses, develop it to be; the context of the major field sets only the loose boundaries. The teaching method, in other words, is a weekly individual tutorial (or, at most, a group conference of two or three students). The trial-major conference teacher, with few exceptions, is

[80] *Bulletin of Bard College, 1942–43*, p. 4.

also the student's adviser. Thus the tie-up between individual study and individual guidance has in the present program been definitely arranged: perhaps the most significant single method toward individual education that the present administration has brought in.

The weekly individual Trial-Major conference for each one of his Junior Division advisees means for the teacher a drain of time and energy which must come from somewhere else in his schedule. It has accordingly been agreed to drop the bi-weekly individual conference in other classes, wherever the teacher feels it necessary.[31] This result of a concession to human limits, it can be seen, tends even more to emphasize the major field as the core of the student's study program.

In the matter of outside courses, the requirement to take a course in each division (the old "sampling" plan, which had crept into Bard during its first six years) has disappeared. Courses outside the major are selected by the student with his adviser's help. The patterns vary with the individual case according, for example, to the gaps shown in his high school record, or to his vocational plans, if any. Despite this individual option, the hope is officially held that the student's spread of course-experience will be broad:

From these exploratory courses the student should see his own activities in relation to those of other scholars and artists. He makes thus a beginning toward a general education.[32]

Finally, in the present administration as in the past, informally arranged instruction—short-term course-work to fill a specific interest or need (such as occasional "hole-plugging" to fulfill a graduate or professional school requirement), liberal use of independent projects and tutorials—in brief, the methods of a free system of teacher-student activity which has been found in the other two colleges—are found to be embraced by Bard, in accordance with its adherence to the aims and methods of individual education. Before the listing of courses in

[31] "Memorandum to the Members of the Faculty," Bard College, October 29, 1940.

[32] Bulletin of Bard College, 1942–1943, p. 8.

each field in the current catalog, the following, for example, is stated:

Since the subject matter for study under the Bard plan for individualized education is based upon the needs and interests of the students in attendance during any particular year, the following list covers only a portion of the materials studied in group seminars or individual tutorials.[33]

Briefly to summarize these developments since the start of Dean Gray's administration, the individualizing methods put forth have been found to fit closely to the working aims of Dr. Tewksbury's original plan. The major in the first two years has been made a bit more tentative by the added prefix "trial"; this trial major has also been geared to individual work by its establishment as a separate course on a tutorial basis. The taking of outside courses has been allowed to follow the individual adviser-student decision. The free use of informally arranged individual and group instruction has been kept and furthered.

b. Methods of vitalizing learning.

At this point the close parallel between the general methods of Bennington and Bard seems manifestly clear enough to allow using the same categories for the points still to be examined in the latter's program. It should not, and does not, follow that the evidence found under those categories will be the same.

(1) Approaches to the unification of knowledge.

A brief look back at the ultimate hopes for a liberal education held out in Tewksbury's original document (above, p. 113) should recall the importance he claimed for directing educational development toward a broad understanding of the culture. Part of this was to be the function of skillful, liberal teaching in guiding the student's pursuit, year by year, of his major field. There was planned also, however, another curriculum device to aid the broadening and unifying process.

---

[33] *Ibid.*, p. 18.

Breadth of intellectual outlook, Dean Tewksbury observed, was worked for in the typical college by a program of survey courses in the first two years. In addition to his thesis of the value of early specialization, he stated his opposition to the introductory survey course as being due partly to [34] "the added danger of cultivating superficiality and diffuseness of mind in the student." His alternative proposition was:

. . . general survey courses organized as *interdepartmental seminars* may be more appropriately taken at the *end* of the college course than at the beginning. Such courses would thus serve as the natural culmination of a student's program of studies.[35]

These seminars constitute serious endeavors, on the part of groups of faculty and students, to correlate and integrate various fields of study in the college curriculum.[36]

The history of what happened to these plans is not known. By the time of Dr. Mestre's administration the toned-down announcement of such seminars implies that their general use, and ambitious purpose, evidently did not stay as a program fixture:

Special seminars are organized in the last two years, as the need arises, for groups of advanced students with common interests and purposes.[37]

No mention of such seminars (although informal equivalents within the various divisions are known to occur) is made in the current announcement.

A second important device for pulling subject matter together which has endured to the present day is the so-called Senior Project. This, actually, was not featured in the original plan, though something of the sort was to be contained in the Senior's "final demonstration" (see section on evaluation, below). It is first mentioned in the 1938 *Bulletin of Bard College*:

[34] Tewksbury, *op. cit.*, p. 5. (Italics mine)
[35] *Ibid.*, p. 8.
[36] *Bulletin of Bard College, 1934–1935*, p. 15.
[37] *Bulletin of Bard College, 1937–1938*, p. 15.

In his Senior Project the student is given an opportunity to demonstrate his power to plan and execute significant work independently. . . . Usually it develops from the student's interests in his major field and extends to include one or more additional fields.[38]

In the present operation of the college the Senior Project is found to vary widely with the individual case, not only in its identity and nature but in its scope and attempts to integrate subject matter. The catalog no longer claims breadth of scope as a general criterion, although one division, natural science, states,

In some cases the project may be a paper . . . dealing quite exhaustively with some aspect of science, usually a subject cutting across the conventional sub-divisions of the field and emphasizing the fundamental unity of all science.[39]

The conclusion, therefore, about methods tried out at the college to approach a life-like unity of knowledge in the curriculum seems to rest where it did at Bennington: since these devices must by college policy be adapted to suit the individual ability and need, the results obtained from such measures likewise must be allowed to vary according to the individual case.

(2) "Activities" and the curriculum.

Once again, the college under study shows an original intention to help bridge the gap between curricular and extra-curricular activities, using the dynamics and spontaneity of the latter to help close this traditional hiatus:

Under the new program, it is not proposed to give the student credits for extra-curricular activities, for the College does not intend to give the student credits at all. It will not be necessary to formalize the student undertakings that are usually carried on outside the curriculum. But extra-curricular activities, so far as possible, will be brought into organic relation with the work which the student is doing in his curriculum.[40]

[38] *Ibid.*, p. 48.
[39] *Bulletin of Bard College, 1942–1943*, p. 17.
[40] D. G. Tewksbury, "An Educational Program for St. Stephen's College," p. 23.

In the first Bard catalog, methods arising from this aim were made more explicit, if only in one general area, namely, the fine arts, music, and drama:

In the new program of the college the arts are regarded as an integral part of the academic curriculum on a par with other subjects. It is believed that the study of the fine arts should no longer be divorced from general culture and relegated to the exigencies of extracurricular activities.[41]

The present administration at the college, needless to say, has carried on this policy toward the arts and their place in education. In the other divisions, moreover, something of the same integration is helped by the decidedly active divisional student discussion clubs (which also elect faculty members): the Economics Club, Science Club, and Writers' Club (representing respectively, the Social Sciences, Natural Sciences, and Literature Divisions). Though the academic connection here is kept closer than is usual, such clubs at Bard, to be sure, are not unique among American colleges. The academic flavor, on the other hand, is somewhat stronger than normal.

(3) Attitude toward vocational preparation.

The fact that Bard is a man's college immediately requires, as in all men's colleges, that reasonable attention must be paid to the ideas of the student about supporting himself after graduation. It does not require, on the other hand, that those ideas be allowed directly to influence the nature of his course of study—as most liberal arts curriculums up to very recent if not current times amply show.

The St. Stephen's program as would be expected embraced the traditional attitude:

Its educational policy is based on the belief that before a man begins work in a professional school or enters commercial or industrial life he should have a thorough general training, designed to make him an accurate thinker, an intelligent thinker, and a man alert both to what the world has thought and done in times past and to what are modern thought and modern problems.[42]

[41] *Bulletin of Bard College, 1934–1935*, p. 31.
[42] *Catalogue of St. Stephen's College, 1933–1934*, p. 9.

Dr. Tewksbury's proposal of the new program, it has been seen, hinged in good part upon the identification of each student's course with his own motivating interests and needs. Reading that proposal and the program of studies in the early Bard catalogs leads to the conclusion that, officially at least, the actual *content* to be used in the curricular ladder for those individual interests remained academic subject matter of a conventional kind. (That the individualized *methods* of handling this subject matter would necessarily tend to "pep up" if not greatly alter this content, has been seen.) It was also stipulated: "It needs to be emphasized, however, that the choice of a field of concentration in college does not necessarily imply the choice of a life career. That question may well remain open during the early years of college." [43]

The current Bard program indicates that this basic reference to liberal arts subject matter of a normal kind has been maintained. A recent exception perhaps is the addition of an Institute for Economic Education,[44] which is participated in mostly by students in the Social Science Division. Some of the innervating content that has come as a result is illustrated:

The first studies have centered in the use of documentary films in economic education. Students participate in the work, cooperating with trained research assistants, or undertaking projects of their own . . . statistical and other methods of social and market research.[45]

(4) The Winter Field Period.

Once again, the specific attention to vocational interests which still is not greatly apparent in the curriculum proper may be expected to get its inning during the winter recess, the organizing and carrying-out of which at Bard is practically identical with the Bennington counterpart. (The system at Bard, however, was, also, part of the original college plan.) In like manner, it was first defined for the student as "field work and general reading connected with his own curriculum." But

[43] *Bulletin of Bard College, 1934–1935,* p. 14.
[44] Funds donated by the Alfred P. Sloan Foundation.
[45] *Bulletin of Bard College, 1942–1943,* p. 24.

the first proposal also pointed out a purpose that has since
come more closely to define the Winter Field Period as it is
now used:

> With the increasing emphasis on the value of field work in various
> courses, moreover, it becomes important to set aside a definite period
> during the college year for work actually in the field. The student
> in college should not be isolated in an artificial world of his own
> apart from the realities of contemporary life.[46]

A list of winter field activities performed by Bard students of
a few years ago illustrates again the type of opportunities capi-
talized during the period: [47] "One student was the guest of a
monastery during his six weeks' field period. Others found
tasks in business houses, investment banks, and brokerage
firms. Art study claimed the attention of three students, and
one young artist took special work in caricature with a leading
Boston artist." [48]

c. Methods of socializing individual education.

The analysis of primary aims for the curriculum at Bard College since its beginning (see above) showed an adherence to
individual-centered, life-centered, and society-oriented aims.
The use of the last word "oriented," seems advised. Although
the statements imply fairly directly the desire of the college to
avoid any possible ivory tower wind-up to the boy's intellectual
outlook, the aims themselves, both originally and now, are not
explicitly society-centered. The reliability of this assertion,
however, seems shaky unless it be bolstered by a study of the
methods that have evolved.

Investigation of the available evidence indicates that society-
turned virtues in the Bard program come to light mainly
through reinterpreting curriculum plans and methods already

---

[46] Tewksbury, "An Educational Program for St. Stephen's College," p. 29.

[47] "The Educational Program of Bard College," *School and Society*, Vol. 45,
p. 569, April 24, 1937.

[48] "The Winter 'Field and Reading' Period of Bard College," *School and
Society*, Vol. 53, p. 365, March 22, 1941.—adds another virtue to the plan:
"a number of students upon graduation have been offered jobs by those who
employed them during the field period."

described. For example: the devices for gaining breadth and unity of learning may also serve to his learning about society and social needs, provided the learning is steered by his teachers in that direction.[49] The New Institute for Economic Education shows potentialities for more real contacts with social problems—if only to the students in its division. The Winter Field Period offers perhaps the strongest force for bringing the learning of students of a rather remote and self-contained college community temporarily at least into the main currents of outside society. All of these potentialities, it must be noted, rest their case here more upon what *may* be done than what ostensibly *is* done in the college's stated practice.

As at the two other colleges, a large degree of student responsibility in community government is officially furthered as a chance to provide "a training school for the principles and practices of democratic government." [50] As at the other colleges also, a necessary high-tuition policy has resulted as yet in less of a range of represented economic groups than was originally hoped for.

The situation of the college in a rural area limits outright chances for college and community collaboration on activities of mutual benefit. The college participates in the Red Hook Community Chest, some of which contribution comes from periodic "main dish-less" dinners in the dining hall. Social education values from this, however, could hardly rate as very rich or enduring. Once again, local defense agencies are providing unprecedented chances for town and gown to work together. It seems evident that such an artificially-made boom may become the basis for some continuing program of cooperative work and activity.

Meanwhile, the tentative conclusion on the whole is that,

[49] Such "steering" is sanctioned in one division at least, Social Science, which states in its announcement of courses (*Bulletin of Bard College, 1942–1943*, p. 23), "These aims and objectives are to help the student acquire (among others listed), a healthy skepticism toward contemporary solutions to social problems accompanied by an incentive to discover more satisfactory solutions based upon a more adequate knowledge; and a sense of civic responsibility which will encourage the student actively to participate in the affairs of adult society."

[50] *Ibid.*, p. 15.

from the foregoing evidence alone, specific aims and methods in the area of social education seem to be less concretely developed in the Bard program than at the other two colleges in this study. This in no sense denies the perfectly possible fact that, in the actual spirit, daily influence, or teaching of its staff, Bard might be doing in this area as much as, more than, or much more than they. If such should be the case, the failure to know it here is due perhaps not so much to the college as to the inevitable lacks in sensitivity of a formal study of this kind.

Evaluation and control.

Writing for a periodical in 1935 Dean Tewksbury listed seven basic points for the Bard College program. Number four was stated:

The student will be expected to assume the chief responsibility for his own education.[51]

Responsibility, Tewksbury believed, could not be expected without accountability. Such accountability was to come at two periods in the four-year course: halfway through, when the student would submit to a "comprehensive review" of his work; and at the end, where he would be asked to make a "final demonstration." Both of these periods were then planned as rather formal evaluations by the faculty, generally assisted by a Committee on Examinations.[52] Examinations, written and oral (including, in the original proposal, outside examiners for the final demonstration—similar to the early Sarah Lawrence plans), thus were to have definite place, although in the Senior Comprehensives the "final demonstration" was left somewhat elastically as "examinations, term papers, or special field work." [53]

At the same time, it is interesting to see that these two

---

[51] Tewksbury, "The Educational Program of Bard College," *School and Home,* Vol. 16, p. 652, April, 1935.

[52] The earliest idea for the Sophomore review, according to the "Blue Document" plan, was "tests will be given in individual cases." However, by the time of the first catalog announcement, this was generalized, for some reason, to apply to all.

[53] *Bulletin of Bard College, 1934–1935,* p. 18.

planned periods of rather formal trial served in some contrast to the rest of the evaluation plans. Aware from the first
of the implications of an individual education, the original
proposal for the college had said, "In the rating of the student's
progress and the evaluation of his final achievement . . . there
will be no arithmetical reckoning of credits. The student's
progress . . . will be considered as an organic whole." [54] To
engineer this latter, the tutorial conference was planned as the
center for a periodic, subjective reporting on how the student
was coming along. Further to implement evaluation in the tutorial, the first catalog included proposed record-forms: for
the student's work sheet which would list for the instructor's
benefit the actual work the student had covered outside since
the last tutorial conference; and also for qualitative "criteria
sheets" to be used by the teacher in submitting to each student's adviser quarterly reports on that student's work. These
devices have remained virtually unchanged to the present day. [55]

A qualitative system of evaluation, moreover, once again
showed itself to be more consistent with the aims of individualized teaching. By the time of the college's fourth year the
general plan of examinations for the "Sophomore Modera-
tions" had been replaced by an advisory committee's decision
on the student's promotion, on the basis of his record plus an
oral interview (in which he gave his plans for the latter two
years). [56] In place of the "final demonstration" in the Senior
year, the Senior Project (see above, p. 137) became the principal datum besides that of his general record for the awarding
of the degree.

[54] Tewksbury, "The Educational Program for St. Stephen's College," p. 11.
[55] The criteria sheet for a given course, listing such items as "understanding
and critical analysis," factual information, skills and techniques, etc., comes from
the course's instructor to the adviser, bearing check-marks for each item, in
each case somewhere along a ten-point linear scale ranging from "failure" to
"outstanding." The result becomes a vertical profile showing various degrees
of achievement in the different aspects of the course. The adviser uses the
profile, plus the evidence from the student's own work sheet, submitted monthly
to him, to prepare his quarterly report of the student's work. Aside from these
technicalities, the evaluation system at Bard is so closely similar to that used
at Bennington (q.v.) that repetition here seems less a virtue than an economy.
[56] *Bulletin of Bard College, 1937–1938*, p. 18.

Continuous with these developments, the present Bard College position on the matter of evaluation is given:

The main criterion throughout shall be the individual development, in terms of the student's purposes and not in terms of some meaningless average. Because of the close contact with the teachers, the development of each student is being evaluated continually rather than at stated examination periods. The faculty has a greater body of evidence of progress or failure than usual and can dispense with artificial tests. The conferring of the degree will represent the faculty's judgment that the student has reached a satisfactory degree of training in one broad field of scholarship and has acquired a satisfactory awareness of the meaning of work in other fields.[57]

Admission policies.

A limiting situation which faced the inauguration of the Bard program in 1934 was the fact that three-fourths of the student body had entered when the school was St. Stephen's. Although no abuse is meant toward the ability and character of these individuals, the original proposal makes it plain that a rather special kind of student would be desired to build up the dynamics of the new curriculum:

Evidence of talent or promise in at least one field of cultural achievement will hereafter be regarded as the primary qualification in the selection of students for admission to the College. In laying aside the insistence upon a group of specified subjects or units applicable to all students, the College is simply carrying out its conviction, which runs through the whole program, that concentration rather than dispersion points the true road to education.[58]

The announced admissions policy accordingly, in addition to the usual provisions about sound record, personality, etc., stated that although generally good records would be welcomed and might largely be the case, the College preferred to find "those applicants, otherwise qualified, who present evidences of marked ability in some broad field of study. . . ."[59]

Again, practical experience has come in time to soft-pedal

[57] *Bulletin of Bard College, 1942-1943*, pp. 10–11.
[58] Tewksbury, "An Educational Program for St. Stephen's College," pp. 5–6.
[59] *Bulletin of Bard College, 1934-1935*, p. 34.

or change this particular aim. Whether the third instance of this sort serves to build up evidence that the normal boy or girl of college-entrance age is not clearly stronger in one "broad field"; whether the measures of this quality, if it does exist, are not reliable enough to be of use to the admissions officer; or whether practical reasons beyond these have come into the picture, the special-field criterion has been removed from the Bard statements.

Instead, an interesting alternative is stated: "An attempt is made to keep as nearly as possible a representative cross section of college youth." [60] The present Bard admissions policy, in brief, officially favors an attempt to collect a student body which will best profit themselves, each other, and the institution by coming to Bard.

CONCLUSION

More than seven years ago a magazine editorial called attention to Bard College and its program, concluding that "The Bard experiment is one more sign of the profound self-searching through which the American educational system is now going." [61] The study of the record of this experiment has yielded the fact that the "self-searching" there has been rather literally true. Throughout three administrations, which, all in all, have held to a remarkable consistency in the primary aims, the college has searched itself continuously in the efforts to find methods more fully loaded to discharge these aims. Around the central method of the four-year major study has been built regularly and informally scheduled tutorials; advanced seminars; field projects and other independent work; pattern of courses assigned according to the student's and adviser's decision; and a varying amount of individuation of course-content (especially in the major study) which nevertheless uses for its basic reference normal academic subject matter in the liberal

[60] *Bulletin of Bard College, 1942–1943*, p. 49.
[61] "Experimental Educational Methods to Be Tried by Bard College," *New Republic*, p. 234, January 9, 1935.

arts. With the apparently successful marriage of methods derived from Bennington to those evolving from the original Tewksbury plan, the college at present is perhaps in its best position to date for the continued work on aims and methods in individualized education.

Chapter VI

The Progressive College Programs:
Conclusions

CHAPTERS III, IV, and V have tried to present, in approximately the same framework, the description of how three separate colleges independently developed their educational aims and methods, from founding until now. Although it proved impossible, for clarity's sake, not to stop and draw comparisons at certain points along the road, the first intention was that each college's career should be shown as a venture on its own.

Now it seems the time to consider systematically whether the use of progressive "college" instead of "colleges" in the study's title can be justified. The task of this short chapter, in other words, is to bring the various points of those three records together to see wherein they do and wherein they do not jibe.

Inasmuch as the discussions in the foregoing chapters have used periodic summaries, with a conclusion at the end of each college's analysis, the entries here may serve best by aiming at briefness and a reasonable objectivity. Unless it is otherwise noted, the following statements are meant to apply to what has been found common among all three of the colleges studied.

AIMS

1. Sarah Lawrence, Bennington, and Bard Colleges came into being to apply systems of modern educational methods to a college program as a whole. Two of these colleges avowedly took these methods from the progressive education movement in America; Bard, though it did not at the outset specifically

avow this, now does so, with a program very little changed in method, none in aim, from its original plan.

2. The main tenet of the college aims is to build a program which in *each individual student case* takes its form according to that student's interests, abilities, and needs. The chief implication of this and all other progressive college aims is to help the student take on the responsibility for his own education.

3. A second main aim is to make college education more vital by taking more of its form and content from present-day life—especially, life as the given student has or has not seen it, and is likely in the future to see it.

4. A third aim is to prepare each student in some way to be an active and intelligent member of our society. This has been less definitely and directly stressed than have the other two aims.

METHODS OF CURRICULUM AND INSTRUCTION

5. *Three levels* of what colleges mean when they say "individualized curriculum" are found. All three are used at these colleges:

a. The student, with advice, may select his own pattern of courses.

b. The teaching *method* is adapted to individual students by use of small conferences, tutorials, independent study and work-projects, and individually defined standards (see Evaluation, below).

c. The *content* of what the student studies, whether within courses or instead of taking courses, is allowed to differ for each individual. This seems to come last in the progress of the college program, and to develop more or less inevitably from the use of the individualized methods just given.

6. The choice by the student of a course-program is nowhere treated as a "free election." The adviser system functions in varying degrees to help him pick those courses which seem best fitted to his nature and purposes.

7. The core of the individual's program at two of the colleges has centered in the four-year pursuit of a chosen major-

study. Sarah Lawrence makes its program "core" a matter of general intellectual development, to be defined in whatever course of study best seems to fit at the given period.

8. Despite the aim toward life-centered education, the essential subject matter studied in the progressive college to date has remained a fairly conventional menu of liberal arts, within four main fields: natural science, social science, literature, and fine arts.

9. The study of the theory and practice of fine arts with full curriculum status and credit toward degree is, however, a feature still in advance of many colleges. As one result, this division has seen an unusual development and occupies a strong place on the progressive college campus.

10. The conventional subject matter is also innervated by certain devices at these colleges toward a more vitalized study, prominent among which are:

a. Special courses, projects, and seminars for the purpose of cutting across and uniting various subject fields.

b. Recognition of extra-class student activities as part of the study program: e.g., plays; chorus; student government; science club; etc.

c. Encouragement of the student to use a vocational interest when such arises for the inspiring and directing of study. There seems, however, no special machinery beyond this for the use of vocational motivation, except:

d. The Winter Field Period for outside, often vocational, project-work, at two colleges; Sarah Lawrence, being near the city, balances this somewhat by frequently assigned short-term field projects.

11. Society-centered education, besides that directly relevant to the Social Science division, is as yet handled for the most part by intra-college activities—housing organization, intramural games, community government, etc. The tradition of large student option and responsibility helps this. Outer-community contacts for educational or cooperative work purposes, meanwhile, is increasing from a rather neutral original position. In the lead of such a growth are the plans at Sarah Lawrence

for an "Institute for Democratic Morale" (tentative title). Social education opportunities in the Bard and Bennington Winter Field Period are apparent, though largely governed by their
appropriateness to the individual case.

EVALUATION AND CONTROL

12. Evaluation at each college started with some intent toward periodic formal tests and objective gradings. The influence of an individualized program has led to the development,
in their stead, of qualitative and subjective ratings, which try
to take in all aspects of the student's response to his work.

13. Thus, examinations, grades, academic honors, and arithmetical credits are not used, except, in the case of the last, to
satisfy State University requirements.

14. The general use of psychological data and insights in the
evaluation and guidance of the student is found to vary. At
Bard and Bennington, this is somewhat minimized in favor of
a relationship between adviser and advisee which centers on
teaching and learning problems. At Sarah Lawrence, the use
of personal and psychological data in teaching relationships
plays a recognized part. Psychiatric help is availed of at all
three colleges when needed.

15. The A.B. degree is awarded upon the decision of a committee which reviews the candidate's total college record, academic and otherwise. No fixed criteria are held, except that,
at Bard and Bennington, proof of competence in the major
field plays a considerable part in the decision. A Senior Project
or Thesis is usually asked for.

ADMISSIONS POLICIES

16. A first policy applied from the start has been the freedom of college, secondary school, and pupil alike from the
bondage of special course requirements for entrance. None is
made.

17. The policy, at each college, started with a requirement
of evident talent in some one field of study or performance.

This disappeared early from Sarah Lawrence, lately from Bard, and is decreasing at Bennington.

It may be asked in the foregoing conclusion why the central topic in this study, general education, was not directly considered. A first answer is that to take up that question now, before the next chapter's evidence is in, would be premature. A more specific answer, however, is that this chapter has tried to present a report of the aims and methods of three colleges *as they were found* to be stated, practiced, or planned; and at only one place in the study was the term "general education" overtly mentioned. The task ahead, in other words, is to examine further evidence toward an answer of what general education in the reference of these colleges seems to mean.

In the meantime, however, the absence of general education from the foreground of discussion at the progressive college is in itself something of a significant fact. It also serves aptly to introduce this chapter's concluding business: a brief summary presentation of the new Bennington program, as initiated in the fall of 1942.[1]

THE NEW BENNINGTON PROGRAM

It may be asked at the outset why the new Bennington program has been separated by two chapters from the rest of the discussion of the college. The first answer is simply that the material was not available on time to go into the rest of the Bennington analysis. Even then it might have been added at the end of that chapter. It was not, for two reasons. First, it represents not a review of what has been, as the other discussions do, but a projection of what is to be—hence it would seem to belong after the conclusions about the records to date. Second, coming where it does, it serves as a useful complement,

[1] N.B. Material for the following was kindly lent by Bennington College, in advance of its publication as the College Announcement for the fall. Because of the manuscript form in which it was received, it will be impossible to give specific page reference. All quotations, however, unless otherwise noted, come from this official college statement.

for the purpose of later discussion, to what has been reported immediately before.

Aims.

A basic recognition will be more definitely made of a two-headed objective for the college program: "Education for citizenship as well as individual development, responsibility as well as freedom, commitment to the values of the cultural tradition as well as cultivation of specialized interest." The present college believes its ten years have developed successful program tools for the fostering of the student's individual development. For her introduction to the culture and her place in it, new techniques, keeping up with the changing needs of the times, are to be added.

Methods of curriculum and teaching.

The primary new device toward introduction of the student toward her culture is the program of "Basic Studies." These consist of a number of coures—twelve at present—taught by regular staff members in the different representative fields. Sample titles are "Political Institutions and Ideas"; "The Western Tradition in Literature and Philosophy"; "The Language of Music"; "The Nature of Physical Science." Their function is described:

The program of Basic Studies provides for the acquisition of an elementary literacy in the arts, sciences, and humanities. The content of the Basic Studies emphasizes the historical development of Western culture, and the ethical and philosophical issues which are of great and continuing importance. . . .
. . . Both the materials and methods of instruction arises out of the experience of ten years in building a curriculum based on the needs and interests of individual students. The faculty have attempted the difficult task of selecting . . . the content which will best serve the common needs of students who must learn to function immediately as active and responsible participants in our society.

The Basic Studies are not planned to be survey courses in, for instance, the University of Chicago sense; for the student they will stress not so much a learning of many facts as learning *from experience* in the various fields. This calls for a continual appeal to active response—discussing, composing, singing, experimenting, measuring, etc.—as a prime teaching method: "In all fields, the aim is to teach students how to deal directly with materials, and how to find their own way as competent workers."

The Basic courses will not be prescribed. Taking a broad pattern of them, however, unless the individual case should show no need, will be generally urged. The student is expected to take one course dealing with the scientific method, and one each in the verbal and non-verbal aspects of the arts.

The other main part of the curriculum will devote itself to "Special Studies." These will concern "the fundamental knowledge and techniques in each of the broad fields of human achievement. . . ." As before, the student with interests in one line may start at once to work in the field or fields which interest her.

In method both the Basic Studies and the Special Studies will be organized as normal subject-matter courses (not including the workshop and studio groups). In the presentation of these courses, the Bennington individualizing methods—tutorial conferences, small discussion groups, project work, etc.— are retained. Contrary to past procedure, in some courses prerequisites are established.

A principal change involves the disappearance of the Trial Major from the first two years. To further this elimination of early high-powered specialization, the academic divisions, as administrative units, have been removed. In the Junior Division, then, the student takes a varying pattern of Basic and Special studies, the latter perhaps in two or more fields. Her work is overseen by her counselor, who will no longer necessarily represent her chief field of interest. When she becomes ready for the Senior Division, her promotion will be contingent on her *whole record* and working interests (although failure to do uniformly well is not held against her) shown throughout. Demonstration of special competence, for its own sake, is not required.

In the Senior Division, six weeks after entrance, she is allowed permanently to select a major study in some field which the College approves as being not too narrow, not too broad. In this she will do half or more of her work, under a teacher who will be called her Tutor. The other half she is expected to use "to continue to pursue interests of a more general nature." Her degree will be awarded her not on one criterion as before, but on two: "This degree is a certificate both of competence in a major field, and of *general education based on the important elements in American civilization.*" [2]

In keeping with these changes, finally, the admissions policy no longer looks for signs of one-line talent; "the emphasis is on encouraging application from any student who will actually gain from the type of education Bennington has to offer."

[2] Italics mine.

Chapter VII

As the Teachers See It

ONE of the reasons why the discussion of the progressive college programs in the preceding chapters avoided claiming any ultimate authority is the relatively "juiceless" sources from which that authority came. A college is not a list of aims and methods in a catalog, nor is it a machine which executes those plans; nor, though often spoken of as "alive," is it an organism, able to act integratedly with a center of experience of its own. Functionally speaking, a college is a group of individuals, living and working as a community; and aims, methods, and results about that community take on final reality only when those particular individuals are held in mind.[1]

This does not mean that a study of a college should aim at finding diversity of action ahead of cooperation and unity. But it may mean that such a study is not judged adequate until it has at least tried to get closer to what is being thought and done at that college than can be gained by merely visiting the campus and reading the available college documents. It should have tried somewhere to appreciate what R. L. Kelly must have meant when he wrote, at the end of a chapter on contemporary college experiments: "The biggest achievement in curriculum building is to set adventurous students among the masters."[2]

The present study was able to go only a few steps in that direction. The "adventurous students" were not contacted, to

---

[1] See F. H. Allport, *Institutional Behavior,* pp. 3–28. 1933. In this chapter Allport does a classic job of reducing mystical social entities—Alma Mater, the State, etc.—to their human elements.

[2] R. L. Kelly, "Remaking the College Curriculum," in *The Effective College,* p. 64. 1928.

any representative degree. Something over a third of the faculty, at each college, were interviewed. With the limits of time and opportunity, the latter were chosen rather than the students, for the reason that this study was approaching the progressive college from the conceptual or *planning,* rather than the evaluative, side (see also Chapter III, p. 49). Thus, the ruling outside question for a program of interviews at the college became not "What are the results?" but *"What thinking about the program, by those largely responsible for planning and carrying it out, is at present going on?"* [3]

Work upon a question of this kind can proceed through a number of channels. It may try to judge ideas from practice, visiting classes and conferences in the effort to collect a large amount of quasi-objective data. It may set up a check-list faculty-questionnaire, adding as many controls, through careful wording, as can be added without destroying the life of the questions. Or it may proceed in a way which might be called clinical: that is, to arrange for a personal conversation with a number of faculty members, in which only the very outside controls are laid down, details and direction being left to the individual instructor visited.

In a context so open to personal values as is college curriculum research, the question of controls and objectivity raises decided problems. Awareness of these problems elsewhere has led to statements ranging from a cautious admission by the American Council on Education that "It is probably true that there are many stimulating and refining inferences in the life of an undergraduate that can never be measured objectively," [4] to the report by Ruth Munroe of Sarah Lawrence, in commenting on their early experience in developing research on admissions, that "the rather subjective rating reached by the admissions committee on the basis of general consideration of all the

---

[3] The administrative set-up has not been included in this study's range. It can be said here that a large degree of faculty participation in curriculum planning and execution is provided for in all three colleges, both through specified committees and general meetings.

[4] American Council on Education, *The Measurement and Guidance of Students,* p. 2. 1933.

materials at hand had a higher predictive value than any of the objective tests used, either singly or in combination." [5]

Should a college study, therefore, try to use methods that will nail down objective and comparable data; or should it seek facts that sacrifice wide comparability in order to gain more lifelikeness and relevance to that particular scene? Answer should depend on what, after all, the particular study is chiefly aiming to learn. In the case of the present study and its hopes, an expert opinion which seemed most pertinent was that of Dean Melvin H. Haggerty, reached after his fifty-seven-college survey for the North Central Association:

. . . One may count the average number of months that a faculty has spent in graduate study; the aims of education are less amenable to arithmetical consideration. . . . In dealing with the less precise elements of education it is desirable to explore what men have thought about them and to assess, by the processes of judgment, the more complex activities and purposes of institutions. This procedure is preferable to applying methods of accurate evaluation to problems they are not fitted to solve.[6]

The method of inquiry accordingly picked for a closer study of the ideas involved in the progressive college programs may be briefly described. Since what was being looked for was *the thinking of individuals now teaching in those colleges,* the best plan appeared to be to go and ask those individuals what they thought. It was not possible to ask them all; eventually forty-eight instructors were interviewed [7] (this does not include eleven non-teaching administrative and personnel officers). The conversations ranged in length for the most part from a half-hour to an hour, although two were for only fifteen minutes, while six lasted nearly two hours. Notes were made in a few cases during the conversation; in all other cases, within three hours after the talk.

All the faculty interviewed at the three colleges had some preparation for the visit. At two colleges, notes containing the

[5] R. L. Munroe, *Teaching the Individual,* p. 42. 1942.
[6] M. H. Haggerty, *The Educational Program,* p. xxvii. 1937.
[7] Respectively, seventeen, fifteen, and sixteen, in the different colleges.

gist of the visitor's study were circulated, with a word about the visitor; at the third college, a member of the staff made the appointments by telephone, introducing the visitor as one making a study of problems of general education in the progressive college. Teachers to be interviewed were first contacted in each case by a member of the administrative staff. By request, no special discriminating factors were used, save that full-time teachers were asked for in preference to those on part-time. It was hoped that a representative sampling of major fields, age, and experience in the school might be obtained, and fortunately it was.

The aim set for the faculty interview was to hear from the teacher the chief values he held for his college's educational system, and the methods he believed in or practiced to help capture those values. In keeping with this aim, no pattern or schedule for the conversation was made ahead of time. No one means of introducing the subject was ever used twice, but rather, as with the ensuing conversation, it was allowed to take its individually determined course. However, once the idea had been presented, in some way, that the visitor was interested in seeing the progressive college teacher's task through his ideas about his job, in the large majority of cases the teacher "caught on," and obligingly opened up his own avenues of discussion. If he did not, questions of fact were usually asked, such as his use of the advisee system; his teaching schedule; procedures used in helping plan a student's course; and so on. Conversation moved easily from these specific points to those teaching and planning questions where choice, belief, and values must play a basic part.[8] The only "steering" that was used, if needed, was to see that the conversation somewhere arrived at a discussion involving what getting a "general education" in that college seemed to mean.[9]

[8] It was explained, of course, that complete anonymity both of instructor and of particular college would be maintained in further use of the material.

[9] (a) In only three cases of the forty-eight did this prove unfeasible. (b) Since, as Chapter II has shown, we cannot yet speak definitively when we talk about general education, the conventional attributes already discussed in this book were used in the approach: "breadth" of learning experience, acquisition of fundamental cultural knowledge, preparation for cooperative social living, etc.

The notes from the forty-eight interviews were rewritten as one- or two-page summaries of what had been discussed. Whenever possible, the interviewee's actual words were used; at all times, nothing but his own expressed ideas were included.

The rest of this chapter will present a summary of the ideas of those forty-eight instructors, as they were learned in individual conference at the respective colleges being studied.

Not everything that was expressed in those conferences appears here. Rather, what is included is the range of thinking on those issues which, without direct solicitation, were brought up by the faculty as being important to the progressive college and its program today.[10]

In the following summaries, according to earlier agreements, names are removed and the three colleges, with the remarks of those of their faculties who were interviewed, are scrambled. It can only be reported at the outset that similarity among the three colleges in the ideas and attitudes of their faculties proved to be every bit as close as the closeness of their programs might suggest. In other words, the evidence gained here seems again to bolster the legitimacy of speaking generically of "the progressive college," so far as these three are concerned.

1. *On the outside, how does the progressive college teacher view his job?* (Mentioned by 17 instructors.)

All but one commenting here expressed a real enjoyment of teaching in the progressive set-up. The most frequently heard comment was "continually stimulating." Others were, "You can teach anything and at any time you like"; "You can see real development in your student"; "The democratic spirit of the community makes you want to do your best work."[11] Two

[10] To a limited extent, perhaps, the cruciality of a question on those campuses may be judged by the proportion of teachers interviewed who brought it up for discussion. Yet this was bound to be skewed by local circumstance: e.g., Bennington, at the time of the visit, was in the midst of discussing the new Basic Studies program. Questions involving the place, use, and standards for subject matter almost inevitably rose to the forefront of conversation.

[11] Quotations in these sections, it should be remembered, are not infallible reproductions of what the instructor said, but come directly from notes made at or just after the interview.

teachers with European teaching backgrounds said the change from the Old World prescribed system was refreshing.

On the other hand, frequently coupled with the comment "stimulating" was the remark that teaching here is hard work, a steady drain on time and resources. This is attributed to the numbers of individual conferences and different courses of study. It loads on a heavy reading schedule to keep up with each student, and keeps the teacher hopping.

This situation led one teacher to say that teaching along so many different topics at once can lead to a certain superficiality, a "talking off the top of one's head."

A young instructor, at the college only a relatively short time, summed it up: "You really find out how to teach, here."

2. *What is the present status of progressive education in the college, according to its teachers?* (Mentioned by 30.)

A variety of attitudes centered in the discussion of where the progressive college stands today. Although, to a degree, almost all of the comments made in the interviews must have some general bearing upon this point, there was a good deal of specific opinion on its status as a body of theory and practice in college education.

The greatest coincidence of opinion (nine) sees the progressive college as having made a chief, and significant, contribution to techniques for promoting *individual development through college learning.* One said it could hardly be called a "system"; it is merely what comes from putting a teacher and student closely together—the rest is up to both. Another opinion was summed up, "Progressive education should be a kind of case-study work, with the academic experience the core of the activity."

Close to the foregoing opinion, six teachers believe "progressive education" comes down more to a matter of individualized teaching method than anything else. To one, it is nothing but "good teaching and common sense." Another gave his belief that it amounts, in essence, to "a highly developed system of tutorials." One instructor linked the progressive college with *all* colleges, whose mission it should be to increase the tribe of "the artist-teacher": the person who sees his chief duty not that of "collecting credits, ticket-taker fashion," but "the task of bringing about, through the use of talents and techniques, creative activity on the part of his students."

Other opinions, each of which occurred in three or more cases were:

The progressive college has a decided place for discipline. It should not pamper students or allow sloppy work.

Restrictions by graduate schools hamper its work.

It needs to get better general agreement on fundamental aims.

The progressive college must not be thought of as merely a center where teachers love students and feel for their welfare. It must have *techniques, system, and equipment* to do its job effectively.

3. *What kinds of methods, large and small, do they favor for the task of individual education?* (Mentioned by 30.)

While the chief aim of the interviews was a discussion of educational ideas, these ideas often have vague reality until they are connected with actual teaching practice. In the majority of the interviews the faculty members found cause to stress certain methods they felt to be especially suited for working out their teaching aims. A report of those methods cited will show a good deal of duplication of the evidence discussed in Chapters III, IV, and V. Some of the teachers, however, described additional pet devices. A retailing of a few of these should be of some general interest:

Once again, the heart of the progressive method, in a plurality of cases, is seen to be the individual conference. This is regarded by several as a sort of springboard for various other teaching purposes: the enrichment of regular-course work; getting to know the student really well; old-fashioned coaching at times; getting "fruitful work out of even a slow learner." Another special use, the broadening of interests, will be mentioned below.

A second group of methods brought up by several (eight) involves the question of how to reconcile individual interests with general subject matter, especially in general introductory courses—a problem about which more must be said further on. The most common answer returns again to the individual conference as a place for molding both the interests and the subject matter. In presenting the material itself in class, however, two interrelated points were often stressed, especially the second:

(1) Building an understanding of *large, unifying concepts* in the field studied should be the aim of introductory-course content—not the learning of arrays of fact.

(2) *Active experience* should be the chief learning method, even in elementary-course work. Workshop and laboratory; writing, composing, reading aloud; singing, painting, constructing; field-tripping, measuring, analyzing, were all used as illustrations, by teachers of the respective fields represented by such activities.

A third of the faculty members discussing special methods mentioned those which aim at broadening students' interests or attitudes, usually through individual conference but sometimes in class. These may best be described by four simple examples:

A student interested in literature but limited by reactionary attitudes towards minorities is expanding under the influence of a specially devised program of reading, including *Native Son* and other stories of the American negro, followed by *The Grapes of Wrath* and other works on struggling economic groups in our society.

Science- and art-inclined students with limited literary backgrounds are offered a special course in Readings in Modern Literature. Each student picks his reading, from a wide list which features literature bearing on science and art aspects of the culture being discussed.

A literature student (for instance) who shows early distaste for social science is advised to take his next literature course with a certain instructor, who habitually approaches literary problems from a social point of view. This is called the "oblique" approach to new divisions of knowledge. It is said often to lead to the student's gladly taking work in the formerly disliked subject, later on.

A French teacher keeps different folders of periodical-clippings in French, bearing respectively upon literature, social science, natural science, and the fine arts. An entering student is invited to prime his [12] French reading by borrowing material from the folder which bears on his chief subject-interest.

To conclude the report on methods, mention of those broached in each case by from two to four instructors may be briefly made:

Teaching even of formal subject matter can be made elastic, year by year, by adapting the *order* of topics presented, according to the interest and ability of the class. In time, all the needed content can be covered this way.

Broad-area courses lose punch if different teachers "shift off." One teacher should carry through.

Contrary to popular belief, there *is* room for formal teaching, including lecturing, in the progressive college.

Group work, as well as individual work, besides being a useful change of pace is coming into its own as a valuable teaching method. It must not be thought that *all* teachings swings on the individual relationship.

4. *How is teaching of the fine arts seen at the progressive college?* (Mentioned by 8 instructors—all the arts instructors interviewed, representing painting, sculpture, drama, and music.)

A special section to consider fine arts teaching is prompted by the significant place these fields have played in the progressive colleges. This does not mean that the arts teacher has come to any special position of authority on these campuses. It does mean that his work is seen with perhaps an unusual degree of interest and sympathy.

In one way or another, these instructors unanimously established one point: that the fine arts in a college of this sort are needed to help show these students what *participation* and *experience* in learning really feel like. There is belief that most of this side, in their backgrounds, has been understressed. One instructor summed it up: "We don't want to turn out professional artists here; we're trying to give them back their hands."

Along with the foregoing, six of the eight referred to the fre-

[12] In order to maintain anonymity, the masculine gender is used throughout this section, whether the reference be to Bard or to one of the two women's colleges.

quent need to break down either of two groups of attitudes which entering students show toward the arts: (1) the stage-struck or dilettante attitudes that the arts are all glamour and fun; or (2) the inferiority feeling that they "can't do anything" in art. The former attitude soon melts under the stress of hard work and gentle-but-firm correction; the latter disappears more slowly perhaps, through the gradual building up of proficiency in the particular medium the student is found best fitted for. One teacher has his beginning students draw with large, free movements on scrap paper for the first one or two weeks, as-suring them that nothing will be kept or shown anywhere.

The second main point discussed by all concerns the use of theory in the arts. With no exception the opinions agree that in the teaching method, theory and practice depend upon each other. One teacher waits, in studio class, until a discussion among students at their work spontaneously develops; then he "moves in." On the strength of such informal treatment, he finds books recommended during the discussion are almost al-ways hunted up and read.

General intellectual values in work in the arts are thought by several to be potent. At one college a course combining painting and philosophy was taught for three years. One of the two teachers who collaborated in it illustrates:

One day, from an idle question on how the world would look to you if you could walk into it through a certain artist's canvas, we developed a discussion of all the major European schools of paint-ing, and the philosophy behind them.

5. *What should be the place of the student's interests in decid-ing the course of his college education?* (Mentioned by 33.)

The importance of the question of "individual interest ver-sus general subject matter" to all concerned with it on the col-lege campus is shown by the fact that forty-one out of the forty-eight instructors voluntarily brought up either one or both sides of the question. (The other side—the subject-matter is-sue—follows this section.) An attitude favoring some checks on the interest motive was one of the commonest features of the faculty interviews. Perhaps this reflects an awareness that unbridled student interests have been made a major point of attack upon progressive education. On the other hand, it may mean an honest confession of difficulty with what has been a hard point to solve in the execution of progressive aims.

To five of those talked with, the interest question is made less serious by the fact that the average student on entering frankly doesn't know what he wants; he is glad to be advised. To eight others, however, reconciling student interest, chiefly in picking the course-program, is a decided problem.

A sizable group (ten) said that, for good or ill, what typically happens in choosing courses is a bargaining between adviser and advisee, in which powers of tactful persuasion play their part. A few frankly stated there is a certain degree of "kidding" the student into taking courses that the instructor feels are for his good.

An equal-sized group defended either these or other acts of teacher option by voicing beliefs that always letting the student decide—such as whether to enter a course for which he does not seem equipped—is harmful to his best interests. Two opposed a high degree of student-option on the grounds that it is poor social education. Three others proposed that picking courses in a field directly opposite to his main interest is, or should be, a stimulating challenge to the student.

With all the above criticisms of the interest motive, nevertheless the largest accord of opinion (thirteen) [13] believes that the use of the student's interest remains the soundest educational basis for the building and direction of his college course. Five of these instructors added what might well serve as the best working compromise of the problem: the use of student interests is all right as a *starting point,* provided the educational course following that choice keeps a balance between his own and other's choices of what he should do and whither he should go.

---

[13] It should be made clear, if it has not been made so far, that of these different opinions more than one were sometimes given by the same person. Thus, the sum of all these opinions necessarily adds up to more than the number of persons who gave them.

6. *What is the place of subject matter in individual education?*
(Mentioned by 27.)

The discussion-summaries on the whole indicate a growing interest within the progressive college in the place of organized content in the curriculum. This does not necessarily mean a corresponding lessened interest in the student. Opinion on the whole matter, as the preceding section shows, is far from settled.

More than two-thirds (nineteen) of the teachers who discussed the question feel there is a place for some kind of organized subject matter in the curriculum, to which individual interests should somehow be adapted. The particular kind of subject matter referred to varied with the instructor and his field. About one half (nine) confined their remarks to their own fields, stressing the need for better coverage of the field; for a more definite sequence of taking courses (as against the idea that a student may take courses in any order); or for "sound content" within certain particular courses. The others of this group mentioned course work and curriculum planning in general as the area of need for the college as a whole.

One representative opinion (seven) is that reconciling general subject matter with individual interests really creates no special problem in the progressive college, *so long as its methods for vitalizing the material and for bringing individual student response are kept in good working order.*

Not necessarily on the opposite side but moved perhaps by different motives, eight teachers brought up points to illustrate their belief that education is, however, primarily a *qualitative* business, i.e., that *what happens to the individual* through the influence of his college course is more important than what books or subjects or formal learning he and his fellows have shared in common during that time. Holders of this belief in most cases followed with the statement that progressive college graduates vary in the amount of formal subject they have covered—some have covered a great deal—, but the average product can handle himself better in an intellectual situation than can the average conventional college graduate. No statistics to prove this, naturally, were offered, beliefs being based in most cases on personal observations.

7. *How can the student in the progressive college be fairly evaluated?* (Mentioned by 16.)

Although only a third of those interviewed brought up the problem of student-evaluation, most of those who did spoke of it as a real issue. The commitment of the college to the individual makes for fine teaching methods; but measuring the product in terms only of his own yardstick is no easy matter.

Discussing the situation, six teachers directly mentioned student evaluation as a major current problem in the college. No solutions were offered, but the feeling seemed to be that somewhat more formal and general methods of evaluation, accompanying a more deliberately organized study-content, may be on the way in.

Five other teachers independently gave support to the above. Their opinions are that, in their several fields, evaluation may in the future become more a man-to-man business, as a result of various trends toward asking students to read more material in common.

A minority vote (three) was given for the use of more examinations, whether objective or essay. This was balanced by the opinion of three others that a program of examinations is not compatible with the progressive college program. One of these added his alternative choice, "plenty of papers." Two other teachers likewise believe evaluation, especially for the degree, may be furthered by submitted evidence of the student's ability to handle himself independently in his major field—specifically, by a Senior Project.

8. *How is "general education" seen at the progressive college?* (Mentioned—more or less on request—by 44.)

The modest listing of this study's title question among the others in this chapter is less in keeping with the aims of this study, perhaps, than with its position in discussion at these colleges. Excepting the present year at Bennington with its new program, general education has apparently not been seen as a "red-hot" issue on the progressive college campus. On the other hand, its problems are in many ways so close to the currently discussed problems on these campuses that in several of the interviews lively discussions evolved, concerning local aspects of the general education question.

On the outside, the evidence from these discussions seems to show that those who are mainly satisfied with the progressive program tend to believe it gives a good general education, which in most cases they interpret as *breadth of intellectual experience and attitude*. They see no essential strife between individual-education and general-education objectives; both, they feel, must imply wide learning experience, and *a growth in the ability to handle oneself in all types of intellectual situations*. In the actual operations which should be performed to meet these aims, however, they typically differ with most of the methods described here in Chapter II.

Those, on the other hand, who are critical of a good part of the present program seize upon general education as a chief virtue that the progressive program "hasn't got." The common complaint is against the one-sided course some students are allowed to pursue, or else against the loose responsibility the students feel for really getting to know the facts of their civilization.

General education as training toward social responsibility came up as an issue in only a few of the discussions. This may have been due partly to the predominantly curricular trend of the conversations, whereas social training is seen by teachers as largely a personnel or all-college matter.

To break down the statements recorded, it appears from this sample evidence that there are some five types of answers given by progressive college teachers to the general education question. This does not mean that each teacher gave one answer and stuck entirely to it. Several gave two or even three during the course of the interview—a fact which may reflect either their open-mindedness on the question, or the difficulty in bringing these elusive matters down to hard and fast points of departure.

a. *The formal answer.*[14] (Mentioned by 9.)

The first type answer to general education in the progressive college points for the most part not toward what is, but what "should be," the case. In its most direct form, it is stated familiarly:

> There is a certain core of information about our society today to which all college students should be exposed. That is partly what a degree in liberal arts should mean.

Five of the nine thus directly faced the issue. Regarding how this should be engineered there was variety of opinion. One accepted the need for a partial return to old-fashioned "prescription of fundamentals." Two of the five, however, as well as all the rest of the instructors in this category, thought that a pattern of integrated and correlated introductory courses might well be taken by all. The feeling was (as in question 6, above) that such a system would do no violence to individual education, provided *experience* rather than just cold facts are stressed, and individual conferences and projects, for all courses, remain the rule. Such methods, it was believed, would distinguish these from "survey courses" in the encyclopedic, Cook's-tour sense, which no one seemed to favor.

When asked how students might be evaluated with such a system, four said that some sort of examinations might become necessary.

b. *The environmental answer.* (Mentioned by 13.)

This category loosely combines two different kinds of ideas which do not necessarily merge. The first idea, common among seven, is that the all-round life, activities, and influence of the college are perhaps stronger agents toward general education than is the curriculum. Specifically mentioned were the regular all-college schedule of lectures and forums; the close con-

---

[14] These categories are the writer's, and need not stand. Examination of the statements under each may enable better ones to be suggested.

tact for the student with his fellows in all sorts of study areas; student activities, such as student government and choral group; and the generally stimulating force of a young, experimental college.

Added to this class of ideas are the suggestions of three that a general educational interest, especially in societal affairs, increases at the college in socially stimulating times—for example, the early years of the New Deal. It is hard, then, at the college not to be interested in the world and society outside.

The second group of ideas with an environmental turn concerns the problem of how to cope with students from rather sheltered homes. Of the six mentioning this problem, two spoke of it only as a teaching issue—a matter of breaking down resistance to new ideas. The other four saw it as a problem in education for social understanding and cooperation.

All the opinions in this rather broad category, then, perhaps collect only about the point that general education is a campus as well as a curricular matter. It is decidedly affected by backgrounds—past and present, immediate and outside.

c. The individual-centered answer. (Mentioned by 23.)

By far the largest proportion of opinions gave, either directly or by implication from the methods they favored, the answer to "general education" which seems most consistent with the aims and methods of these progressive colleges. Briefly summarized, this view is that a *general education,* like any kind of education, *is defined by the individual human learner.* There is no such thing as a "general general education"; that area of learning which may mean breadth, or preparation for society, to one learner is so much wasted time and motion to another. That the student should not be allowed to study just one thing is uniformly agreed by this group. But what other things he should study besides, they feel, is a matter for his own nature and aptitudes, as seen by himself and his teachers, to decide.

The type of program planning which comes from this view typically consists of the choice of one or more major interests;

these are then built out by other course choices which seem to harmonize. When possible, the picture of the career he plans is used to help choose the subjects. If the student graduates without having studied physical science, for instance, opinion varies as to the degree of fault in this. The staunch supporters of the individual view say, in his case, the fault is less than it would have been had he been ordered willy-nilly to take it. A subtler answer proposed by two teachers (which points toward type "e," below) is that by good planning and teaching, the science-evading student could have taken a course in another field with a teacher who would present, *through the medium of that field,* useful essentials of the scientific method. This may, of course, be easier to say than do.

d. *The "compromise" answer.* (Mentioned by 10.)

Close to the individual-centered opinion is one which, however, keeps a finger on an outside obligation. This obligation is the traditional belief that a generally educated person should at some time have studied in the humanities, the fine arts (though this has come recently), the natural sciences, and the social sciences.

The conventional way to insure this coverage would be the old group-sampling plan (see Chapter II), applied to the first two years. In these colleges, it is more elastically handled. The student, at the outset, is encouraged to spread his choices as far as he will. A course or field which is objected to may be laid aside perhaps until the junior or senior year, by which time it is often found that his resistance to it has been outgrown. Study in some neglected field, moreover, is sometimes arranged for a student on a short-term, tutorial basis. In the case of meeting graduate school requirements, this occasionally becomes officially necessary.

e. *The "liberal" answer.* (Mentioned by 17.)

A more descriptive title for the fifth center of opinion on general education might be the "unity-of-knowledge" answer. Two main sub-types of attitudes may be described.

The first group of opinion under this heading stems from the claim of the progressive college that the aims of education for the individual are qualitative. Such a position, to this group, means that *what* the student studies in college makes relatively little fundamental difference. The purpose and method of the college should be to make the most of each individual as a developing rational human being; and this process should use whatever field of study seems best adapted to that purpose. Several instructors stressed that great range and quantity of material is not necessary to this task. *"One course* may open the world to him," was one suggestion. Another told of a great teacher who had developed lessons in many fields of knowledge from the single observation of a leaf falling to the ground. A third said that his experience in writing a thesis in graduate school had been more of a "general education" to him, in the sense of learning to find knowledge and organize thinking, than any courses of study he had ever taken. Several offered illustrations of the "general education" they believed to be inherent in a truly rich study of their one field.

As a second main group, seven teachers of this "liberal" class of thought did not go so far as to sanction one field of study *per se* for achieving all the virtues of a general education. Rather, they looked toward a system of teaching so elastic that the student, with expert guidance, might cover all the main fields and disciplines of learning through the medium of *one main course of study.* The machinery for this would demand broadly conceived courses; constant individual attention; easy cross-overs to the facilities of other fields; frequent short-term help from other teachers; and instructors "who teach from an underlying conviction in the philosophical approach to learning." Some degree of the "unity of knowledge" might thus become functionally possible in the college program.

Although the thinking of this group of teachers seems closer to the ideal than the real, they believe that to some degree these ideals have actually been made reachable in the program of the progressive college. The impression, moreover, is hard to deny that it is these particular teachers who must have done much to bring about that possibility.

CONCLUSION

The teacher in the contemporary progressive college is not a professional genius, unique among American college teachers. He is not a crank on the subject of individual-centeredness in the college curriculum. He is aware of the changing emphases of the times, which today means, particularly for him, a slow but definite shift from preoccupation with individuality to a balance point somewhere between the individual and his embattled society.

Like all teachers, the progressive college teacher believes in the value of his particular field, for him and for his students. This leads him, especially in critical times, to worry whether this college system really allows one to feel sure that the students are "getting the stuff." This has led in turn to a certain number of moves in the direction of more formally arranged learning experience at the college. Nevertheless, to an almost unanimous extent, he believes in the assumptions of the progressive college, and is therefore mindful of his obligation to "teach students, not subject matter"; and to help develop in those students disciplines which will come primarily not from externals, but from themselves.[15]

[15] These last two summary beliefs come likewise from two of the faculty interviews.

Chapter VIII

Summary and Interpretation

INTRODUCTION

As THIS last chapter is being written the world which at intervals we called civilized rocks about our ears. Nations that said "Never again" and told their youth the same are finding they did not end the last war in ways which might make this possible. Thus they work under the burden of having to retrain a generation half-educated for peace in ways of killing other young men almost completely educated for war.

In the press of events like these it is hard for a student of general education in the progressive college at times not to feel that he is doing what Robert Lynd quotes Auden as saying, "Lecturing on navigation while the ship is going down." [1]

Circumstances, however, work to change that feeling at least to some degree. As the invaders drive them from city to city, the Chinese carry their universities, along with their war machinery, strapped to their backs. England keeps her colleges going, profiting from the teachings of the last war about what truly constitutes national resources. America has been urged to profit by the same lesson.

Concretely, although the signs now seem to point to a long war, it becomes apparent that some kind of education in America for grades, high school, and college will keep on. This is seen necessary not only for maintaining our intelligence and morale in the present, but for laying a base to our hopes for a post-war world in which not only general killing but general want may systematically be lessened if not made to disappear. Some of these hopes have entered into the shaping of aims to-

[1] R. S. Lynd, *Knowledge for What?*, p. 3. 1939.

ward giving a better "general education" in the colleges. It cannot be a total coincidence that the stress on this feature of college education has increased at the same time with the rise in national attention, as a whole, toward the problems of working out the slacks and bulges in our form of democratic government.

Starting a few years earlier than the "general education" movement, and prompted by motives surely as broad as if less directly social than those above, a group of elementary and secondary schools in America set themselves to try out on a school-wide basis the best of modern evidence on how educating the child should be conceived and carried out. After a time it was natural that some one should take up these same ideas to be tried on the college level. The schools, and the colleges which they later inspired, came to be called "progressive," and were furthered in their aims by the Progressive Education Association, founded in 1918.[2]

Yet when schools and colleges commit themselves to keeping up with contemporary evidence about education, they have to hold their structures ready for periodic change. The change that is called for today by the pressure for national solidarity, social mindedness, and the kind of "general education" that these imply, on the outside at least would seem to hit the progressive schools hard. For progressive educators, as is widely known, based a great part of their techniques for vitalizing education upon adapting it to the unique demands of each individual learner. This might or might not imply a conflict with the newer, society-centered aims.[3]

An initial interest in the colleges of the progressive type has led the writer to form a study to find how these colleges have approached the problems of individual *and* social education, as well as the other problems which the widespread demands for

[2] These statements at present may be guaranteed only by popular avowals of the Progressive Education Association, since no documented history of its movement is as yet available. One such has been begun, but war activities have intervened.

[3] B. H. Bode, in *Progressive Education at the Crossroads*, 1938, argues that it is a conflict, which so far progressive education has not gone far towards solving.

general education have laid on. To make the study it seemed necessary to enter in and follow through most of the college's curricular program and then draw out the relevant parts from within, rather than to try to fish out the general education implications from the outside. Also, it was felt that "general education," whatever it means, may imply a good deal more than a mere segment of the over-all educational beliefs and practices of the college. The evidence, so far as it has gone in this report, has tended to bear out that feeling.

The task of this concluding chapter, then, is to review the evidence in a way that will show more clearly where the progressive college programs stand in their efforts to meet the current aims of general education. A first thing to do, therefore, should be to look once more at what those general education aims are.

THE GENERAL EDUCATION AIMS RESTATED

In Chapter II it was found (p. 35) that college educators have agreed in focusing their aims, for the purpose of clearing their methods, on two centers, the individual and society. For both they have grouped aims which have been somewhat roughly divided here into quantitative and qualitative aims. In terms of the individual, the quantitative aims call for his effective introduction to a broad range of more or less academic learning about the world and its different subject-fields. The qualitative aims point toward the gradual development of all his personal powers, mental and otherwise. For society, the quantitative aims point toward the student's coming to learn the major facts and problems about his national and world social milieu. The qualitative social aims are split in two closely connected parts: (1) on the immediate scene, the growth in ability to understand and get along constructively with his fellows; and (2) on the broad scene, the growth in abilities and desires for intelligent cooperation in the efforts to improve democratic society.

A fair complaint may be made here that these aims threaten

to defeat themselves by chopping the individual up into five or six inert pieces. Although a certain amount of artificial separation of aims seems necessary as a start for the building of any system of discrete methods to meet them, some condensation of the above may indeed be called for, in order to help this chapter try to wind up rather than unwind some of its outstanding problems. A digestion of the objectives just stated, accordingly, reveals three main directions taken by the body of general education aims. In summary, they seek methods which will help the student grow, in:

1. *Individual development,* of an over-all personal (including intellectual) kind.
2. *Knowledge,* not only of the academic fields of learning but of his current social scene and its problems.
3. *Concern,* for others' situations, interests, and welfare, and for the progress of his society as a whole.

Before discussion goes further, it seems wise to call in an outside caution regarding how far the fulfillment of these aims may be hoped for. Once again, the statements listed were made to apply not to a paper category, or to a mechanically improvable machine, but to the highly fallible and distractable eighteen-year-old. Any reference to "results" in the remarks to follow should be seen with this underlying human limitation in mind.

THE GENERAL EDUCATION AIMS AS SEEN IN THE PROGRESSIVE COLLEGE

Individual development.

That the student brings not just his mind but his whole individuality with him into the classroom is something wise teachers knew centuries before a part of modern "organismic" psychology experimentally found it out.[4] At present this fact

[4] J. F. Dashiell, "Contributions to Education of Scientific Knowledge About the Psychology of Learning," *The Scientific Movement in Education,* N.S.S.E. Yearbook No. 37, p. 404, 1938: "Learning is not the building up of highly specific and fixed pathways, but the reaching of some new equilibrium in that dynamic field called the nervous system."

is almost universally claimed by colleges to furnish one of the foundation stones of their programs. Yet just what kind of methodological structure to build on that stone has been a puzzle not yet widely solved. A look back at the various general education plans reviewed in the second chapter may be a reminder that "treating the whole personality" was the aim most lightly treated by the concrete curricular schemes. Instead, the common solution has been to attach a counseling service in some way to the program and trust that, between the teaching and the counseling, the student's personality will somehow receive its due. But this admits defeat to the extent that the college then does administratively what it has just agreed is psychologically unreal—namely, to treat the intellectual branches of the student separately from their personal roots.

This problem of how then to reflect administratively the oneness of the individual learner has inspired reams of earnest discussion and plans. Most of it, though not all, has been on the elementary and secondary school levels. Agreement on all levels seems reached on one point, which was expressed in the late New College's catalog: "Integration is something *within the individual,* something that takes place when his life is animated by purpose and he has the ability to focus his experience on that purpose." [5]

If integration, both in the student and in the college method, is to be helped through centering the student on a purpose of his own, then the progressive colleges have made strong moves in that direction. They have tried to find each student's purpose for him by building his curriculum upon his interests as they appear at the time of his entrance in college. Following that, they have worked toward keeping their treatment of his various needs functionally intact through the use of four chief methods: (1) The actual core of what he studies is largely defined by his interests and carried out semi-independently. (2) The most important part of his course work, for the four years,

[5] Teachers College Bulletin, *New College Catalog for the Sessions 1937–1938.* See also, T. Hsi-en Chen, "Toward Integration," *Journal of Higher Education,* Vol. 12, June, 1941.

is done with the teacher *who also is his counselor.*[6] (3) The personal, administrative, and academic facts about him all clear through his adviser, who also, as his chief teacher, is largely responsible for evaluating his work. (4) The activities and campus life of the student are, to a considerable extent, taken into his guidance and evaluation in the teaching process.

"The student," to·quote again a phrase already reported, "becomes the educational unit of the college."

This program has not gone unchallenged. Aside from its apparent expense, it has been criticized on at least two counts. One is that such attention to student interests—"whims" is the word often used—distorts his social perspective. It emphasizes only "individual needs," soft-pedaling the needs of society. Another implies that it is prodigal; student needs do not have to be treated in such clinical fashion. In his review of President Warren's book *A New Design for Women's Education,* one writer points out the latter view:

President Warren has emphasized the individual and an individual curriculum for each student. Theoretically this is possible —and I believe rightly so—but consideration of the inevitable life activities of American women of today and tomorrow will reveal that there are some *common to all* (he lists here several, involving areas of health, social relations, aesthetic enjoyment, etc.).[7]

Views such as this one are widespread, leading in some cases to curriculums based upon "common" areas like those Robertson refers to. As to the strength of such plans, this discussion has not been and will not be concerned. There does seem need, however, to clear one point on what an "individual curriculum" actually means. It applies to controversies involving both the criticisms of the progressive program just mentioned, although one, the social, will be further treated later on.

Many critics of the "student interests" program, who pro-

[6] This will not be so definitely arranged in the new Bennington program. Judgment must be reserved as to how greatly the change, here and in other areas, will swing the Bennington aims and methods away from those of the other two colleges.

[7] D. A. Robertson, "Another New Dealer," *Journal of Higher Education,* Vol. 11, p. 452, November, 1940.

pose instead a curriculum into which many common needs of that age will be treated, have erred in taking for a philosophy what is in reality a group of methods. In doing this, they miss the distinction between what is content and what is method in a college program. Accept the fact that the content of a curriculum can be built up of common needs of modern adolescent Americans, as Robertson mentions above. Well and good; but what then is the *method of adapting that curriculum to each individual adolescent* who takes that same curriculum? Is it a program of courses? Are there regular individual conferences? How are results evaluated? Are the same books read by all? Is the content allowed to be broken up and approached in different ways, to recognize the fact that *each student has his unique problems within those "common needs"?*

The progressive college, contrary to some popular opinion, has not canonized the student's interest by making it the actual context of his study. As a matter of fact the context [8] of that study, as we have seen, has remained chiefly—too much, perhaps—conventional liberal arts subject matter. It is the *method* that is individualized—that is, the means of assuring that whatever the student "takes" of the given subject matter, and the ways he "takes" it, is shaped to *fit his own way* of responding to a learning situation.

Likewise, we may speak of "society's needs" as proper context for our college curriculum, and this seems eminently right. Yet we do not instruct an entity called "society"; the student is still the only medium we have of getting across the society needs. And to say that these needs should be part of his context of study still is not to deny that this can be most effectively done by designing our method of presenting that context *in terms of the individual learner's situation.*

The conclusions as to the context of study in the progressive college programs will be taken up in the next two sections. In

---

[8] Some confusion between this discussion and earlier ones (e.g. Chap. III) may be cleared up by the distinction between "content" and "context." While it is true that the *content* of the progressive college student's study—or, "what he takes"—is often defined by his interests, the *context* of that content remains, as stated, mainly academic liberal arts subject matter.

the meantime, it appears from the evidence that the individualizing methods of that program have gone further than any
other discernible type of college method in their efforts to
achieve integration of the whole student in the learning process. If such is of first importance to individual development,
as opinion seems to agree, then it can be hoped that this part
of the progressive program, meeting well one general education aim, will remain and prosper.

Knowledge.

"Individual development" to some means so much that it
crowds out any great concern over what more formally should
go into an education. The influence of psychoanalysis and its
offspring upon education—particularly the less sex-centered
and more individual-centered schools of Adler and Jung [9]—has
been to argue that a personally integrated individual is strong
enough to make up for almost any other, more external deficiencies that he may have. In the early years of progressive
education, this view, along with perhaps a too-literal acceptance
of the activity principle in learning, led to a relatively planless
kind of experience which critics were quick to call intellectual
anarchy. Those early trials have generally settled into more established way; still, the subject matter-versus-individual question, despite John Dewey's clarifying *Interest and Effort in
Education* as far back as 1913, remains an operational problem.
That its operations still need to be solved, especially on the
subject matter side, was pointed out, again by Dewey, as recently as 1938 in his fruitful series of lectures bound under the
title *Experience and Education.* Emphasizing that just any
sort of learning experience won't do, Mr. Dewey has told us
(p. 101), "No experience is educative that does not tend both
to knowledge of more facts and entertaining of more ideas and
to a better, more orderly arrangement of them."

Leaning more heavily perhaps on beliefs such as this than on

[9] See A. Adler, *Understanding Human Nature,* 1927; and C. Jung, *The Integration of the Personality,* 1939.

the fact that Mr. Dewey also says here he has taken it for
granted that (p. 113) "education . . . both for the individual
learner and for society must be based upon . . . the actual
life-experience of the learner," college curriculum-builders
have recently attempted in certain ways to present to their students a "better, more orderly arrangement" of facts about the
world. The assumptions that they make in doing this are primarily two: (1) there are certain bodies of facts and principles
about this world which all students should come to know; (2)
these bodies of facts and principles, the college in question is
equipped to distinguish, organize, and teach.[10]

To study the two assumptions now would lead this discussion far astray. In the absence of such study, they are accepted
here as reasonable, with two reservations advisedly made:

(1) Investigation of the various subject matter plans presented by colleges which work on these above two assumptions
leads the observer to wonder just *which* bodies of facts and
principles it is which everybody should come to know. Failure
to agree on this among the different programs is almost unanimous. It therefore seems necessary to say that what facts and
principles are judged essential to general education *will be defined in part by the opinions of those who build the program.*

(2) A study of college programs and faculties as a whole very
often shows (except at large universities) that one college is
"strong" in certain fields and tends to stress them particularly,
while another college has a "wow" of some other department,
and plays this up accordingly.[11] For the majority of our institutions, then, it seems evident that the bodies of essential facts

---

[10] J. R. Brumbaugh, in "The Case For Prescription," *Current Issues in Higher
Education,* ed. by W. S. Gray, p. 44, 1937, gives the position in essence: ". . . Certain fundamental needs requisite to citizenship, home life, health, recreation,
and communication are common to all members of the group. The principles
and experiences essential to satisfying these needs constitute the basic content
of the curriculum. In the relationship of basic content to the common needs of
students is found a sound justification for prescription."

[11] L. O. Perrigo, "The Specialization of the Small College," *Journal of Higher
Education,* Vol. 12, February, 1941, reports, after a study, that hardly any "well-
balanced general colleges exist," and concludes (p. 92): "It is apparent that the
respective administrators and faculties are consciously or unconsciously adjusting
their institutions to circumstances beyond their immediate control."

and principles to be presented to all will be further defined in some part *by the teaching facilities of that college.*

Having defined, prepared, and presented its curriculum of essential facts and principles, some colleges apparently feel that their problem of general education has been for the most part solved. Such a feeling is not consistent with the usual reach of college aims. It is one thing to define general education as the taking of a list of special courses prepared by the college; but it seems a more important thing to define it not only by the catalog list, but by what happens during the process of bringing those courses and the student together. In other words, we are back at the old question of how methods actually meet aims.

If the combined agreement of psychologists and educators since 1900 can be taken as a fair norm of truth, it can be said by now with some confidence that a program of material to be learned can be presented with greatest hope of effect through establishing two conditions in the individual learner: one, that he be allowed to follow his natural impulse to *respond actively* in the learning situation; [12] two, that what is presented to him be made to seem *important to him.*[13] Logically, in order to secure both conditions, the second should probably be arranged before the first.

The presentation of one same broad curriculum to all the students can, if cleverly handled, arrange for a certain degree of active student response—through papers, projects, discussions, etc.—and a feeling on the part of all that it is important to their individual lives. It manifestly is impossible, however, for that curriculum to bring active and individual-centered response from *all* the students to *all* parts of its offerings. (The frank admission of this fact leads some educators to claim an "exposure" to the facts of the world is all that can be generally expected.) As was referred to in the preceding section, a college, after studying its clientele, can build a single curriculum

[12] See footnote, p. 167.

[13] J. Dewey, *Interest and Effort in Education,* p. 43; 1913: "Genuine interest, in short, simply means that a person has identified himself with a certain course of action."

based upon "the needs of the modern individual at X College." But it obviously cannot build a single curriculum based upon "the individual needs of each of the two hundred (or ninety or one thousand) individuals at X College." As for inspiring universally active response: at one college recently a well-established survey course on modern society was voted by the graduating seniors to have been "the dullest course they had taken in college." Aside from the high unreliability of Senior Polls, some cue here may lie in the fact that survey courses and their kind are typically highly organized by the teachers before presentation, in order that the course may vitally reproduce the social scene. Curiously enough, one result is that when this highly organized material is presented, some students tend to be left passive to the performance. All the real thinking—the "correlations and integrations" which teachers prize so highly—has been done for them! [14]

It thus becomes apparent that the bodies of essential facts and principles—the "general education program"—which have been defined, first by the way the college selects them, and second by its facilities for teaching them, must undergo a final redefinition before they reach their mark in the student's developing mind. They must, thirdly, be defined *by the way he himself is constituted to react to them.*

The progressive colleges admittedly have started at the other end of the picture. With the belief that the student's definition of general subject matter is the one which is most important, they have up till now more or less officially disregarded the first two processes above and have begun with the student instead. Where they have ended—that is, how far out into different fields of general and formal knowledge they have led him—has been found typically to vary with the individual case. As a means of keeping him alive and at work, this approach has already been favorably discussed in the present chapter. As

[14] Frank concern is admitted here that the new Basic Studies program at Bennington may, willy-nilly, come to have somewhat the same passive effect. Contradiction of such fears may lie in their bias toward active, first-hand experience and individuality in the student's response, and in their methods for promoting these virtues.

to whether it guarantees the spread of knowledge (or of attitude toward knowledge) that is being asked for in these times, disagreement at the colleges themselves, and trends toward some change, has been seen.

If the progressive colleges in the next few years act (as Bennington, for one, has already acted) toward a more formally organized subject-matter curriculum, it may be because seasoned experience has proved to them that a program starting almost entirely upon the student's interest cannot be made to meet the current aims toward a general knowledge. On the other hand, it may be because they have not fully tried the potentialities of the various methods within their grasp. For in view of the evidence presented up to this point, the reconciling of a strong individual interest with a broad range of knowledge does not on the outside seem impossible, *provided* the kind and degree of response to that "broad range" be yet measured *in the individual's terms.* Such in any case, it was argued above, is inevitable to a certain degree.

One way to do this is being tried at Bennington this next year. This way involves entrance of the student in a number of broad-field courses, during which time she also takes work in fields of her current special interest.   As such, the system does not seem to differ greatly in its outside approach from the conventional college.   Its retained individualizing teaching methods, on the other hand, should serve to keep some essential link with its past.

Another way to match individual interest with general-knowledge aims was originally proposed by the head at one progressive college and has been implied at the others.[15] This plan keeps faith with the earlier progressive programs in that, once again, the core of the student's program at beginning is his chosen major field. It does not leave him there, however. Rather, with the expert teaching that the plan calls for, the individual is to be led, *through the medium of his major subject,* gradually into its broader aspects, first within the field it-

[15] In Chapter V it has been briefly described as Dean Tewksbury's "tree" analogy. Dr. Tewksbury left Bard before it had been fully implemented.

self, later into its relations with other fields. (This particular time sequence, probably, would vary greatly with each case.) The aim would be to move in this way into an integrated learning experience in all the main subject fields; but how far this might go, and how richly into each, must depend on the teachers, the subject, the college facilities, and the student.

A program such as described would not be what critics of the progressive college have called "a planless plan"; it would not face the student each year with a "Well,-what-would-you-like-study-now?" It would instead offer him the supporting structure of a recognized major field, giving him the impetus toward following as rich a course for four years through that field, and into others, as he finds himself able to take in. If his major interest changes it does not ruin the program, but merely gives him another home base, or central pole, for his operations.

This plan has several potent implications which in turn lay demands upon the particular situation where it is to be tried. Since it is in essence a quest in learning, it calls for students who have at least an outside interest in an active, ever-expanding type of college learning. Second, since an elastic program like this is much harder to carry out than a formal one, it calls for the best of adaptive *yet planned* teaching programs' which might include: sound courses which still supply mainly the context, leaving the development to the students and teachers; scheduled tutorial, project, and other individual work, balanced by a more truly cooperative kind of group study; cross-over classes and seminars between fields; and so on. Third, since it thus implies a good deal of belief in *the ultimate unity of knowledge,* it calls for teachers, not necessarily gifted in research, but endowed with more than average insights into what teaching and learning are fundamentally for. Authoritarians or academic isolationists could quickly wreck a program of this kind.

Two remaining implications of such a plan carry considerations beyond the particular college scene. First, as it may have been observed, the plan would not discharge the general educational aims for a spread of knowledge within the first two years. In fact, it appears probable that under this program the student might not approach fulfillment of those aims (even in his own terms, to which this discussion persistently holds) until his third or fourth year. By this, then, general education becomes not the business of any prescribed number of years, as some current trends favor, but of *the whole of whatever length of time the individual is able to spend at his education.* There seems no reason to believe general education should not continue into graduate study, if any, or into life itself, provided facilities for some forms of implementation happily remain at hand.

From this directly comes the second implication, concerning the difference between "general" and "special" education. So far as to distinguish one type of course, or course-group, from another course, such a distinction has shown its uses. Yet under the plan proposed above, the actual operations and results of "general" and "special" study can be seen to be interdependent and relatively indistinguishable. What student can say, after two months of studying corporation history, or Freud, or molecular physics, just when he has gained strictly special, when strictly general values? If the evidence and logic in this discussion can be accepted as sound, in other words, general education becomes not an entity, nor any certain "part" of education, but rather *a kind of value, or attribute, in the overall educational process itself.*[16] It is, perhaps, a different value from liberal education only in the sense that it has usually been thought of by its college-educator employers as something they can "put into" the program; to that degree it become quasi-operational, whereas "liberal" is often thought of as one of the happy end-results of the educative process. General education, moreover, being a fairly recent term, can be thought of as involving learning drawn not only from the liberal arts, but largely from everyday life and living as well.

If such a view of general education has the real basis that the discussion argues, it becomes apparent that the progressive colleges, as now constituted, do have the potentialities for build-

---

[16] This may help to explain the writer's *sub rosa* difficulty, throughout the study, in separating general-education aims from aims for education in general.

ing methods toward a more general knowledge into their programs.

First, however, there is one more region of general education aims which must be reviewed.

Social concern.

A strong individual development, according to some people, removes most of the need for worry about that individual's formal learning, so far as general education is concerned. Somewhat comparable to this, a large body of opinion has favored, and still does, the view that a broad knowledge about society is in itself the guarantee of social responsibility and concern. The liberal arts colleges have traditionally upheld such a belief; as a matter of fact, many of these still take pride in the fact that "pure learning" is the keystone of their arch.

Contemporary society has become less patient with pure learning. The standards for social responsibility have risen so that broad knowledge in itself no longer seems able to furnish a strong guarantee. As Robert Lynd says (and what he addresses to one field he would doubtless expand to include all teaching), "A world floundering disastrously because of its inability to make its institutions work is asking the social sciences: 'What do you know? What do you propose?'" [17]

In the current rise in educators' work toward meeting the heightened social aims, some overswing has been more or less inevitable. Thus we hear, in schools and colleges, new courses on Democracy, and whole sections of a college program have in instances been reoriented toward a literal translation of loyalty-to-democratic-aims into the formal course of study.

Aside from forgetting certain principles of teaching-effectiveness, there seems some danger that courses of this kind may tend in their zeal to blur the distinctions between totalitarian and democratic relationships of the individual to his society. In the current waves of enthusiasm it is hard, and yet is it not essential, to remember that democracy seems to function best on the basis, not of the primacy of the individual, *or* of the

[17] Lynd, *op. cit.*, p. 7.

primacy of society, but on the basis of the establishment of an *implemented working relationship* between them.[18]

Whatever the truth of the last statement, however, it still leaves the schools and colleges with the job of gearing concrete aims and methods toward building such working relationships for their students, as they prepare for life outside.

Returning to the progressive colleges, the sum of the evidence gained is that they seem to be doing neither greatly less nor greatly more of a job in social education than is the average contemporary college.[19] It may seem surprising, for instance, that the faculty interviews show a rather modest interest in the problem of seeing their college program in relation to the demands of broader social scene.

A major part of this, it should be explained at once, is due to the fact that the interviewer's first purpose, on each campus, was to learn those faculty ideas based primarily on the most important stated aims of their particular college. To challenge them with questions from the outside scene would have been interesting, but it was not feasible. In the short time allowed for each talk, it was perhaps inevitable, then, that the more concrete and obvious matters of individual teaching and subject matter should have crowded out discussion about the ultimate social reference for such items, especially since clearing the former matters was specifically needed for this study. On the other hand, this may reflect, in some way, the rank such issues hold on those campuses. These colleges started as eager ventures to try new methods in vitalizing and individualizing college learning. Aims concerned with giving a social reference to the methods were not strong charter members of the original programs. In the background, shaded by the enthusiasm over those methods during the intervening years, the larger, social

---

[18] The individual-society debate has been featured by straw men; or, as Dewey says (*The Public and Its Problems*, p. 69. 1927.), "We might as well make a problem out of the relation of the letters of an alphabet to an alphabet. An alphabet *is* letters, and 'society' *is* individuals in their connections with one another."

[19] Here it must be warned again that the personnel policies of the colleges, undoubtedly potent forces in social education, have been covered in this study only to the extent to which they merged with the educational program itself.

aims have grown slowly. Meanwhile, the strong aims and methods surrounding individualized study, having featured the program from the start, still serve chiefly to characterize it now.

Nevertheless, the social aims are there to be built upon. It is apparent from the outside that they could stand more definite attention within the colleges. One way to do this may be through periodic self-study of *all* the college's objectives, as the results of Bennington's recent self-evaluation seems to show. Another way, which is gradually coming to be accepted at the college level, is through the deliberate training *and selection* of teachers in terms of the long-range as well as short-range objectives of their jobs. A few years ago such an idea for college teachers would have been heretical; but now the defenses against it are not so sure.[20]

Can the progressive college, then, move in a social-centered direction more definitely than it has? Critics who say it cannot, as presently constituted, believe that a program which takes its working definition from the individual learner cannot consistently adapt that definition to a broader reference. Yet this belief implies that the progressive college as a whole has made the individual interest not only the method but the philosophy of its program. Such is not the writer's opinion. The opinion to the contrary is partly based on observations, reported in this study, that the progressive college, without giving up its faith in individual methods, *is* gradually modifying both aims and methods toward a more concrete social concern. Like almost every other college in America, it has miles to travel in this direction.

If the above observations are right they may in time be strengthened by evidence of further progress in two areas already alive on the progressive campus. These may be briefly mentioned and underscored:

(1) *Campus life.* One widespread opinion among students

[20] By way of analogy only, the work of the recent cooperative study group at Columbia University who for a year studied "The Role of Colleges and Universities in the Education of Teachers for the Modern Secondary School" seems fruitful. Something like this may in time be done for teaching in the Modern College.

of college personnel problems today is that social education, like any other kind of education, grows chiefly through student experience in its various phases. Again, it is the job of the college to organize that experience in some way.

The fringe of evidence on the progressive college campus life that has been reported here points to a self-contained college community where the student's share in life and government is encouraged to be high. It points also, however, to the fact that the student's degree of option regarding the extent to which he shall take part in that life and government is also rather high. Current trends in campus organization are showing a growing belief that while the former fact is essential to real self-development in democratic living, the latter may actually get in its way. It may be, in other words, that giving the student an active role in the running of his community should be put less on an optional basis, for his own and others' benefit. By this no coercion is proposed. Rather, what is meant is a more definitely geared and oiled campus organization, in which everyone has some chosen contributive role, large or small. Although all copies and comparisons of college plans are dangerous, The Community Plan at Antioch, at least by concrete operations in this area, seems to be leading the way.

(2) *Outside contacts.* The original aims at each of the progressive colleges called for "life-centered learning." Whether this was meant to refer to the student's life or to life in general is not entirely clear. Reference to the student's life was made sure by projects, tutorials, and the other forms of individualized learning. Reference to life in general became realized through generally vitalized subject matter, field projects, and longer-term off-campus work, such as the Bennington and Bard Winter Periods, and the Yonkers housing survey conducted at Sarah Lawrence. The stress of present events has led to a considerable growth in more sustained outer-community contacts in general. The Bennington Survey, regional defense work at all three colleges, and the Sarah Lawrence plans for a permanent community institute combine to show concrete signs toward an implemented social education on the larger scene. It

may be that the current crisis will serve the progressive college a permanent good turn in terms of its own aims, by showing it what, in the realm of activities beyond the campus grounds, "life-centered learning" can mean.

GENERAL CONCLUSIONS

In 1931 Dean Max McConn expressed the opinions of more than just himself when he called for a college which would actually build its whole program upon the principle that the student will learn meaningfully that which he sees in a truly close relation to himself. Such a hypothetical college, he believed, would have three distinguishing features: (1) an admissions policy based on perceiving intellectual interest, not certified course-credits; (2) a policy of student advisement which "would really be taken seriously"; and (3) a curriculum which the teachers would have full power to build around each individual student, and to change as that student changed. Dean McConn concluded, "I think it not unlikely that within the next twenty to fifty years some institution will find the courage and means to adopt some such plan as a whole." [21]

The prediction did not have to wait so long. In that same year Sarah Lawrence changed its experimental two-year junior college into a four-year institution, based in part upon the exact principles that Dean McConn had publicly prayed for. The next year Bennington started its version of the same practices and beliefs. Bard in 1934 added a third example. During the next ten years these colleges carried on persistent activities of experimentation to show that an interest-motivated curriculum did not have to wait any longer in American educational history to be successfully tried.

In recent years new demands, as always, have come up from the changing outside scene. Programs which based themselves on individual-centered education find that the demand is now more deliberately to prepare that individual to think less in terms of himself and more in terms of his society. Society wants a citizen whose capacities to help it have been enhanced

[21] M. McConn, "The Problem of Interest at the College Level," *Progressive Education*, Vol. 8, p. 684, December, 1931.

by "a general education." This in turn asks that his personality, his knowledge of past and present, and his interests be adapted more in terms of those "general" standards.

The adaptation of the progressive programs to such new demands, the foregoing discussion has proposed, can be done. It can be done, furthermore, without destroying either individual education or the general standards. This belief has come from two main conclusions from the evidence presented:

1. General education, as an operation in the educative process, ends not as a thing, or as a body of knowledge, but as a value; and it is defined differently for each individual who comes to possess that value.[22]

2. The chief contribution of the progressive college to date is the furnishing of methods by which the individual of college age comes to see drive and meaning in his study. The progressive college has seen the individual's interests as the starting and guiding point for his education. It has not necessarily seen those interests as context or end-result of the process. If and when it does so (as temporarily it may) it does itself harm, for it then loses its best chances to adapt its methods to other, broader, ends.

In its need for a more conscious journey toward these "other, broader ends," the progressive college, because of its peculiar method, may indeed have a special task. That method has given us an approach to the learner which seems too good to lose. May society not ask the progressive college, and others taking up its work, in time to help show if it can how its methods can be shaped toward a new concept of human relations, expressed thus by Thomas Mann: "In the future, international life, like the national life of the peoples, must be ruled by a new concept of freedom as a socially integrated and limited individualism." [23]

---

[22] To the question, for instance, "How can a person be called generally educated when he has never studied the tax system?" the answer suggested here is, "A generally educated person is one who knows when he needs to know about the tax system, and goes and learns about it."

[23] T. Mann, "How To Win the Peace," *Atlantic Monthly,* Vol. 169, p. 182, February, 1942.

To assign even a part of this tremendous chore to a small college, trying to give its students their money's worth of liberal education, seems at once unreal. The task there too, however, amounts to a fundamentally kindred problem: *how to adapt learning to the individual pattern, and yet fit that individual pattern into some broader, organized plan.* To say that the progressive colleges have not solved their problem very completely seems no more nor less fair than to say modern democracy has not yet solved its own.

A final word of qualified regret seems called for, for having made a study which to the alive and busy progressive colleges themselves may seem like something of a vivisection. This study has been an attempt to see how the educational program looks from the point of view of the planner, of the person who, with three hundred years of American college education behind him, a vague but needy clientele before him, and over a thousand other going college "plans" on all sides of him, must decide or help to decide what the program of *his* college shall be.

Since this has been such a kind of study and not an evaluation of results, it has not been the place here to speak of the seventy-books-per-year-per-pupil average circulation of the libraries; of the startlingly mature work products; or of the testimony of those who come from visits there saying such things as "The plan works; the campus seethes with ideas. . . ." It *is* in keeping with this study, however, to end by saying that in the writer's opinion the strength of the ideas behind the programs is such that they will endure; and that however the progressive colleges produce methods to match their aims in the next few years, the process should be an engrossing one for us all to witness.

References

I. GENERAL

(Chaps. I, II, VII, and VIII)

ADLER, A. *Understanding Human Nature.* Garden City Publishing Co., Garden City, N. Y., 1927.

AIKEN, W. M. *The Story of the Eight-Year Study.* Adventure in American Education, Volume I, Harper and Brothers, New York, 1942.

ALBERTY, HAROLD. "Progressive Education—Its Philosophy and Challenge." *Progressive Education* (Supplement), May, 1941.

ALLPORT, F. H. *Institutional Behavior.* University of North Carolina Press, Chapel Hill, 1933.

AMERICAN COUNCIL ON EDUCATION. *The Measurement and Guidance of Students.* Williams and Wilkins Co., Baltimore, 1933.

ANTIOCH COLLEGE BULLETIN. *Catalog Issue, 1941–1942.* Yellow Springs, Ohio.

BODE, B. H. *Progressive Education at the Crossroads.* Newson, New York, 1938.

BOUCHER, C. S. and BRUMBAUGH, A. J. *The Chicago College Plan.* The University of Chicago Press, Chicago, Revised Edition, 1940.

BROWN, K. I. *A Campus Decade.* The University of Chicago Press, Chicago, 1940.

BRUMBAUGH, J. R. "The Case for Prescription." In *Current Issues in Higher Education* W. S. Gray (edr.). The University of Chicago Press, Chicago, 1937.

BULLETIN OF THE ROCHESTER ATHENAEUM AND MECHANICS INSTITUTE. *Individualized Education.* Rochester, New York, December, 1937.

BULLETIN OF THE UNIVERSITY OF MINNESOTA. *General College of the University.* Minneapolis, 1940–1941.

BUTTS, R. F. *The College Charts Its Course.* McGraw-Hill Book Co., New York, 1939.

COFFMAN, LOTUS D. *The State University: Its Work and Its Problems.* University of Minnesota Press, Minneapolis, 1934.

CHARTERS, W. W. "General Survey Courses." *Journal of Higher Education,* Vol. 13, pp. 1–4, January, 1942.

COBB, STANWOOD. "The New Quarterly." *Progressive Education,* Vol. I, pp. 3–4, April, 1924.

DASHIELL, J. F. "Contributions to Education of Scientific Knowledge about the Psychology of Learning." In *The Scientific Movement in Education,* National Society for the Study of Education, 37th Yearbook,

(G. M. Whipple, edr.). Public School Publishing Co., Bloomington, Ill., 1938.

DEWEY, JOHN. *Experience and Education.* The Macmillan Co., New York, 1938.

——. *Interest and Effort in Education.* The Riverside Press, Cambridge, Mass., 1913.

——. *The Public and Its Problems.* Henry Holt and Co., New York, 1927.

EDMAN, IRWIN. *Philosopher's Holiday.* The Viking Press, New York, 1938.

EDUCATIONAL POLICIES COMMISSION. *The Purposes of Education in American Democracy.* National Education Association, Washington, D. C., 1938.

EELLS, W. C. *Surveys of American Higher Education.* Carnegie Foundation for the Advancement of Teaching, New York, 1937.

FRASER, M. G. *The College of the Future.* Columbia University Press, New York, 1937.

GIDEONSE, H. D. *The Higher Learning in a Democracy.* Farrar and Rinehart, New York, 1937.

GRAY, W. S. (edr.). *General Education: Its Nature, Scope, and Essential Elements.* The University of Chicago Press, Chicago, 1934.

——. *Provision for the Individual in College Education.* The University of Chicago Press, Chicago, 1932.

HAGGERTY, M. E. *The Educational Program.* The Evaluation of Higher Institutions, Volume III. The University of Chicago Press, Chicago, 1937.

HSI-EN-CHEN, T. "Toward Integration." *Journal of Higher Education,* Vol. 12, pp. 307–310, 346, June, 1941.

HOOVER, HERBERT. "Resume." *The University and the Future of America,* Leland Stanford Junior University. Stanford University Press, Stanford University, Calif., 1941.

HOPKINS, L. T. and others. *Integration: Its Meaning and Application.* D. Appleton-Century Co., New York, 1937.

HUTCHINS, ROBERT M. "Hutchins Urges Degree Revision." *The New York Times,* Section 2, p. 5, Sunday, March 1, 1942.

——. *The Higher Learning in America.* Yale University Press, New Haven, Conn., 1936.

JOHNSON, B. LAMAR. "General Education Changes the College." *Bulletin of the Association of American Colleges,* Vol. 24, pp. 228–234, May, 1938.

JOHNSON, B. LAMAR (edr.). *What About Survey Courses?* Henry Holt and Co., New York, 1937.

JUNG, C. *The Integration of The Personality.* Farrar and Rinehart, New York, 1939.

KELLY, R. L. *The American Colleges and the Social Order.* The Macmillan Co., New York, 1940.

——. *The Effective College.* Published by the Association of American Colleges, New York, 1928.

—— and ANDERSON, R. E. "The Extent of the Divisional Development of the Curriculum." *Bulletin of the Association of American Colleges,* Vol. XIX, pp. 418–424, December, 1933.

KENT, RAYMOND A. (edr.). *Higher Education in America.* Ginn and Co., Boston, 1930.

LEARNED, W. S. and WOOD, BEN D. *The Student and His Knowledge.* The Carnegie Foundation for the Advancement of Teaching, Reprinted from Bulletin No. 29, New York, 1938.

LLOYD-JONES, ESTHER. *Social Competence and College Students.* American Council on Education Studies, Series VI, Vol. IV, No. 3, Washington, D. C., 1940.

LYND, R. S. *Knowledge for What?* Princeton University Press, Princeton, 1939.

MANN, T. "How to Win the Peace." *The Atlantic Monthly,* Vol. 169, pp. 176–183, February, 1942.

McCONN, M. "The Problem of Interest at the College Level." *Progressive Education,* Vol. 8, pp. 680–684, December, 1931.

McGRATH, EARL J. "The Cooperative Study in General Education." *Junior College Journal,* Vol. 9, pp. 500–506, May, 1939.

MEIKLEJOHN, A. *The Liberal College.* Marshall Jones Company, Boston, 1920.

NATIONAL SOCIETY FOR THE STUDY OF EDUCATION. *Changes and Experiments in Liberal Arts Education.* 31st Yearbook, part 2 (Guy M. Whipple, edr.). Public School Publishing Co., Bloomington, Ill., 1932.

——. *The Scientific Movement in Education.* 37th Yearbook (Guy M. Whipple, edr.). Public School Publishing Co., Bloomington, Ill., 1938.

——. *General Education in the American College.* 38th Yearbook, part 2 (Guy M. Whipple, edr.). Public School Publishing Co., Bloomington, Ill., 1939.

NEWLON, J. H. *Education for Democracy in Our Time.* McGraw-Hill Book Co., New York, 1939.

"New Teachers for The New School." A Report of the Cooperative Study Group conducted by Barnard College, Columbia College, and Teachers College at Columbia University. New York, 1942. (Mimeographed.)

North Central Association of Colleges and Secondary Schools. "Manual of Accrediting Procedures." (Mimeographed.) 1934.

OGAN, R. W. "College Programs of Self-Examination." *Journal of Higher Education,* Vol. XIII, pp. 229–235, May, 1942.

OLIVET COLLEGE BULLETIN. *General Information.* Vol. 39, Olivet, Mich., April, 1940.

PERRIGO, L. O. "The Specialization of the Small College." *Journal of Higher Education,* Vol. 12, pp. 89–92, February, 1941.

RAINEY, HOMER P. *How Fare American Youth.* A Report to the American Youth Commission of the American Council on Education. D. Appleton-Century Company, New York, 1938.

ROBERTSON, D. A. "Another New Dealer." *Journal of Higher Education,* Vol. 11, pp. 452–453, November, 1940.

St. John's College, Catalogue for 1941–42. Annapolis, Md.

SCROGGS, S. "Some Factors in General Education." *Journal of Higher Education,* Vol. X, pp. 147–152, March, 1939.

SULLIVAN, L. H. *The Autobiography of an Idea.* Press of the American Institute of Architects, Inc., New York, 1924.

TEACHERS COLLEGE BULLETIN. *New College; Catalog for the Sessions 1937–1938.* Teachers College, Columbia University, New York.

TUNIS, JOHN R. *Was College Worthwhile?* Harcourt, Brace and Company, New York, 1936.

UNIVERSITY OF BUFFALO BULLETIN. *The College of Arts and Sciences.* Vol. 30, Buffalo, N. Y., February, 1942.

——. *Reports of the Chancellor and the Comptroller.* Buffalo, N. Y., November, 1935.

UNIVERSITY OF CINCINNATI BULLETIN. *Cooperative Courses, College of Engineering and Commerce, 1942–43.* Cincinnati, Ohio.

VAN HISE, C. R. *Inaugural Address at the University of Wisconsin.* Madison, Wisc., 1904.

"What Constitutes a Progressive College?" *Bulletin of the Association of American Colleges,* Vol. 19, pp. 108–109, March, 1933.

WHITMAN COLLEGE CATALOGUE. Walla Walla, Wash., 1942.

Whittier College Bulletin, 1940–1942. Whittier, Calif.

WRISTON, H. M. *The Nature of a Liberal College.* Lawrence College Press, Appleton, Wisc., 1937.

II. THE PROGRESSIVE COLLEGES

A. SARAH LAWRENCE

COATS, M. "A New Type of Junior College." *Journal of the National Educational Association,* Vol. 18, pp. 5–6, January, 1929.

COATS, M. "Sarah Lawrence College Statutes of Instruction." (Mimeographed.) Bronxville, N. Y. 1927.

DOERSHUCK, B. "Statement." *Bulletin of the Association of American Colleges,* Vol. 19, pp. 109–115, March, 1933.

MUNROE, R. L. *Teaching the Individual.* Columbia University Press, New York, 1942.

MURPHY, L. B. *Psychology for Individual Education.* Columbia University Press, New York, 1942.

RAUSHENBUSH, E. *Literature for Individual Education.* Columbia University Press, New York, 1942.

Sarah Lawrence College. "Faculty By-Laws, revised as of June, 1941." (Mimeographed.)

——. "Memorandum on the Sarah Lawrence College Institute for Democratic Morale." (Mimeographed.) April 24, 1942.

——. "Outline of Courses For 1941–1942." (Mimeographed.)

Sarah Lawrence College Catalog. 1927–1928.

——. 1930–1931.

——. 1931–1932.

——. 1934–1935.

——. 1936–1937.

——. 1941–1942.

WARREN, C. *A New Design For Women's Education.* Frederick A. Stokes Company, New York, 1940.

——. "President's Report on the First Ten Years of Sarah Lawrence College." (Mimeographed.) 1936.

——. "Self-Education: An Experiment." *Progressive Education,* Vol. 11, pp. 267–270, April–May, 1934.

——. "The Sarah Lawrence Plan." *Nation,* Vol. 131, pp. 549–550, November 19, 1930.

——. "The Sarah Lawrence College Plan." *School and Home,* Vol. 16, pp. 659–663, April, 1935.

B. BENNINGTON

"Addresses Delivered at the Colony Club, New York City." (Mimeographed.) April 28, 1924.

BENNINGTON COLLEGE. *Announcement* for the Years 1932 to 1942, inclusive.

"Bennington College." *School and Society,* Vol. 34, p. 223, August 15, 1931.

BROCKWAY, T. P. "The Community in a Social Studies Program: The Bennington Survey." *Middle States Association of History and Social Science Teachers; Proceedings,* pp. 62–64, 1939.

FOWLIE, W. "The Bennington Experiment." *The French Review,* Vol. 11, pp. 93–101, December, 1937.

GRAY, C. H. "Recess For Work Experience." *Occupations,* Vol. 14, pp. 5–9, October, 1935.

HERRING, H. C. "Bennington." *Nation,* Vol. 137, pp. 651–652, December 6, 1933.

——. "Education at Bennington." *Harper's,* Vol. 181, pp. 408–417, September, 1940.

LEIGH, R. D. "Bennington Gets Under Way." *Progressive Education,* Vol. 9, pp. 370–372, September, 1932.

———. "The Newest Experiment in American Higher Education." In *Higher Education Faces the Future* (P. D. Schillp, edr.). Horace Liveright, New York, 1930.

PARK, F. F. "A Study of the Junior Division, 1937–1938." Bennington, Vt. (Mimeographed.)

The Educational Plan For Bennington College. Bennington College Corporation, revised edition, 1931.

"Bennington College." *School and Society,* Vol. 34, p. 223, August 15, 1931.

C. BARD

"Amended Charter of Bard College as of July 1939." Annandale-on-Hudson, New York. (Typescript.)

BARD COLLEGE. "Memorandum to the Members of the Faculty." (Mimeographed.) October 29, 1940.

BULLETIN OF BARD COLLEGE. 1934–1943 inclusive.

———. *The Bard College Plan For Individual Education.* March, 1940.

Catalogue of St. Stephen's College, 1933–1934.

Committee on Academic Freedom and Tenure. "Bard College." *Association of American Professors Bulletin,* Vol. 21, p. 595, December, 1935.

"Experiment in educational methods to be tried by Bard College." *New Republic,* Vol. 81, p. 234, January 9, 1935.

FAIRBAIRN, R. B. *Intellectual Education in Small Colleges.* Opening address to the students of St. Stephen's College, 1880.

GRAY, C. H. "First Report to the President of Columbia University and the Board of Trustees, Bard College." *School and Society,* Vol. 52, p. 456, November 9, 1940.

LEIGH, R. D. "Final Report to the President and Trustees of Bard College." (Mimeographed.) 1940.

TEWKSBURY, D. G. "An Educational Program For St. Stephen's College"; A Preliminary Statement Submitted For the Consideration of the Board of Trustees of the College. 1934.

———. "The Educational Program of Bard College." *School and Home,* pp. 650–653, April, 1935.

"The Educational Program of Bard College." *School and Society,* Vol. 45, p. 569, April 24, 1937.

"The New Four-Year Plan at Bard College." *School and Society,* Vol. 52, p. 456, November 9, 1940.

"The Winter 'Field and Reading' Period of Bard College." *School and Society,* Vol. 53, p. 365, March 22, 1941.

AMERICAN EDUCATION:
ITS MEN, IDEAS, AND INSTITUTIONS
An Arno Press/New York Times Collection

Series I

Culver, Raymond B. **Horace Mann and Religion in the Massachusetts Public Schools.** 1929.

Curoe, Philip R. V. **Educational Attitudes and Policies of Organized Labor in the United States.** 1926.

Dabney, Charles William. **Universal Education in the South.** 1936.

Dearborn, Ned Harland. **The Oswego Movement in American Education.** 1925.

De Lima, Agnes. **Our Enemy the Child.** 1926.

Dewey, John. **The Educational Situation.** 1902.

Dexter, Franklin B., editor. **Documentary History of Yale University.** 1916.

Eliot, Charles William. **Educational Reform: Essays and Addresses.** 1898.

Ensign, Forest Chester. **Compulsory School Attendance and Child Labor.** 1921.

Fitzpatrick, Edward Augustus. **The Educational Views and Influence of De Witt Clinton.** 1911.

Fleming, Sanford. **Children & Puritanism.** 1933.

Flexner, Abraham. **The American College: A Criticism.** 1908.

Foerster, Norman. **The Future of the Liberal College.** 1938.

Gilman, Daniel Coit. **University Problems in the United States.** 1898.

Hall, Samuel R. **Lectures on School-Keeping.** 1829.

Hall, Stanley G. **Adolescence: Its Psychology and Its Relations to Physiology, Anthropology, Sociology, Sex, Crime, Religion, and Education.** 1905. 2 vols.

Hansen, Allen Oscar. **Early Educational Leadership in the Ohio Valley.** 1923.

Harris, William T. **Psychologic Foundations of Education.** 1899.

Harris, William T. **Report of the Committee of Fifteen on the Elementary School.** 1895.

Harveson, Mae Elizabeth. **Catharine Esther Beecher: Pioneer Educator.** 1932.

Jackson, George Leroy. **The Development of School Support in Colonial Massachusetts.** 1909.

Kandel, I. L., editor. **Twenty-five Years of American Education.** 1924.

Kemp, William Webb. **The Support of Schools in Colonial New York by the Society for the Propagation of the Gospel in Foreign Parts.** 1913.

Kilpatrick, William Heard. **The Dutch Schools of New Netherland and Colonial New York.** 1912.

Kilpatrick, William Heard. **The Educational Frontier.** 1933.

Knight, Edgar Wallace. **The Influence of Reconstruction on Education in the South.** 1913.

Le Duc, Thomas. **Piety and Intellect at Amherst College, 1865-1912.** 1946.

Maclean, John. **History of the College of New Jersey from Its Origin in 1746 to the Commencement of 1854.** 1877.

Maddox, William Arthur. **The Free School Idea in Virginia before the Civil War.** 1918.

Mann, Horace. **Lectures on Education.** 1855.

McCadden, Joseph J. **Education in Pennsylvania, 1801-1835, and Its Debt to Roberts Vaux.** 1855.

McCallum, James Dow. **Eleazar Wheelock.** 1939.

McCuskey, Dorothy. **Bronson Alcott, Teacher.** 1940.

Meiklejohn, Alexander. **The Liberal College.** 1920.

Miller, Edward Alanson. **The History of Educational Legislation in Ohio from 1803 to 1850.** 1918.

Miller, George Frederick. **The Academy System of the State of New York.** 1922.

Monroe, Will S. **History of the Pestalozzian Movement in the United States.** 1907.

Mosely Education Commission. **Reports of the Mosely Education Commission to the United States of America October-December, 1903.** 1904.

Mowry, William A. **Recollections of a New England Educator.** 1908.

Mulhern, James. **A History of Secondary Education in Pennsylvania.** 1933.

National Herbart Society. **National Herbart Society Yearbooks 1-5, 1895-1899.** 1895-1899.

Nearing, Scott. **The New Education: A Review of Progressive Educational Movements of the Day.** 1915.

Neef, Joseph. **Sketches of a Plan and Method of Education.** 1808.

Nock, Albert Jay. **The Theory of Education in the United States.** 1932.

Norton, A. O., editor. **The First State Normal School in America: The Journals of Cyrus Pierce and Mary Swift.** 1926.

Oviatt, Edwin. **The Beginnings of Yale, 1701-1726.** 1916.

Packard, Frederic Adolphus. **The Daily Public School in the United States.** 1866.

Page, David P. **Theory and Practice of Teaching.** 1848.

Parker, Francis W. **Talks on Pedagogics: An Outline of the Theory of Concentration.** 1894.

Peabody, Elizabeth Palmer. **Record of a School.** 1835.

Porter, Noah. **The American Colleges and the American Public.** 1870.

Reigart, John Franklin. **The Lancasterian System of Instruction in the Schools of New York City.** 1916.

Reilly, Daniel F. **The School Controversy (1891-1893).** 1943.

Rice, Dr. J. M. **The Public-School System of the United States.** 1893.

Rice, Dr. J. M. **Scientific Management in Education.** 1912.

Ross, Early D. **Democracy's College: The Land-Grant Movement in the Formative Stage.** 1942.

Rugg, Harold, et al. **Curriculum-Making: Past and Present.** 1926.

Rugg, Harold, et al. **The Foundations of Curriculum-Making.** 1926.

Rugg, Harold and Shumaker, Ann. **The Child-Centered School.** 1928.

Seybolt, Robert Francis. **Apprenticeship and Apprenticeship Education in Colonial New England and New York.** 1917.

Seybolt, Robert Francis. **The Private Schools of Colonial Boston.** 1935.

Seybolt, Robert Francis. **The Public Schools of Colonial Boston.** 1935.

Sheldon, Henry D. **Student Life and Customs.** 1901.

Sherrill, Lewis Joseph. **Presbyterian Parochial Schools, 1846-1870.** 1932 .

Siljestrom, P. A. **Educational Institutions of the United States.** 1853.

Small, Walter Herbert. **Early New England Schools.** 1914.

Soltes, Mordecai. **The Yiddish Press: An Americanizing Agency.** 1925.

Stewart, George, Jr. **A History of Religious Education in Connecticut to the Middle of the Nineteenth Century.** 1924.

Storr, Richard J. **The Beginnings of Graduate Education in America.** 1953.

Stout, John Elbert. **The Development of High-School Curricula in the North Central States from 1860 to 1918.** 1921.

Suzzallo, Henry. **The Rise of Local School Supervision in Massachusetts.** 1906.

Swett, John. **Public Education in California.** 1911.

Tappan, Henry P. **University Education.** 1851.

Taylor, Howard Cromwell. **The Educational Significance of the Early Federal Land Ordinances.** 1921.

Taylor, J. Orville. **The District School.** 1834.

Tewksbury, Donald G. **The Founding of American Colleges and Universities before the Civil War.** 1932.

Thorndike, Edward L. **Educational Psychology.** 1913-1914.

True, Alfred Charles. **A History of Agricultural Education in the United States, 1785-1925.** 1929.

True, Alfred Charles. **A History of Agricultural Extension Work in the United States, 1785-1923.** 1928.

Updegraff, Harlan. **The Origin of the Moving School in Massachusetts.** 1908.

Wayland, Francis. **Thoughts on the Present Collegiate System in the United States.** 1842.

Weber, Samuel Edwin. **The Charity School Movement in Colonial Pennsylvania.** 1905.

Wells, Guy Fred. **Parish Education in Colonial Virginia.** 1923.

Wickersham, J. P. **The History of Education in Pennsylvania.** 1885.

Woodward, Calvin M. **The Manual Training School.** 1887.

Woody, Thomas. **Early Quaker Education in Pennsylvania.** 1920.

Woody, Thomas. **Quaker Education in the Colony and State of New Jersey.** 1923.

Wroth, Lawrence C. **An American Bookshelf, 1755.** 1934.

Series II

Adams, Evelyn C. **American Indian Education.** 1946.

Bailey, Joseph Cannon. **Seaman A. Knapp: Schoolmaster of American Agriculture.** 1945.

Beecher, Catharine and Harriet Beecher Stowe. **The American Woman's Home.** 1869.

Benezet, Louis T. **General Education in the Progressive College.** 1943.

Boas, Louise Schutz. **Woman's Education Begins.** 1935.

Bobbitt, Franklin. **The Curriculum.** 1918.

Bode, Boyd H. **Progressive Education at the Crossroads.** 1938.

Bourne, William Oland. **History of the Public School Society of the City of New York.** 1870.

Bronson, Walter C. **The History of Brown University, 1764-1914.** 1914.

Burstall, Sara A. **The Education of Girls in the United States.** 1894.

Butts, R. Freeman. **The College Charts Its Course.** 1939.

Caldwell, Otis W. and Stuart A. Courtis. **Then & Now in Education, 1845-1923.** 1923.

Calverton, V. F. & Samuel D. Schmalhausen, editors. **The New Generation: The Intimate Problems of Modern Parents and Children.** 1930.

Charters, W. W. **Curriculum Construction.** 1923.

Childs, John L. **Education and Morals.** 1950.

Childs, John L. **Education and the Philosophy of Experimentalism.** 1931.

Clapp, Elsie Ripley. **Community Schools in Action.** 1939.

Counts, George S. **The American Road to Culture: A Social Interpretation of Education in the United States.** 1930.

Counts, George S. **School and Society in Chicago.** 1928.

Finegan, Thomas E. **Free Schools.** 1921.

Fletcher, Robert Samuel. **A History of Oberlin College.** 1943.

Grattan, C. Hartley. **In Quest of Knowledge: A Historical Perspective on Adult Education.** 1955.

Hartman, Gertrude & Ann Shumaker, editors. **Creative Expression.** 1932.

Kandel, I. L. **The Cult of Uncertainty.** 1943.

Kandel, I. L. **Examinations and Their Substitutes in the United States.** 1936.

Kilpatrick, William Heard. **Education for a Changing Civilization.** 1926.

Kilpatrick, William Heard. **Foundations of Method.** 1925.

Kilpatrick, William Heard. **The Montessori System Examined.** 1914.

Lang, Ossian H., editor. **Educational Creeds of the Nineteenth Century.** 1898.

Learned, William S. **The Quality of the Educational Process in the United States and in Europe.** 1927.

Meiklejohn, Alexander. **The Experimental College.** 1932.

Middlekauff, Robert. **Ancients and Axioms: Secondary Education in Eighteenth-Century New England.** 1963.

Norwood, William Frederick. **Medical Education in the United States Before the Civil War.** 1944.

Parsons, Elsie W. Clews. **Educational Legislation and Administration of the Colonial Governments.** 1899.

Perry, Charles M. **Henry Philip Tappan: Philosopher and University President.** 1933.

Pierce, Bessie Louise. **Civic Attitudes in American School Textbooks.** 1930.

Rice, Edwin Wilbur. **The Sunday-School Movement (1780-1917) and the American Sunday-School Union (1817-1917).** 1917.

Robinson, James Harvey. **The Humanizing of Knowledge.** 1924.

Ryan, W. Carson. **Studies in Early Graduate Education.** 1939.

Seybolt, Robert Francis. **The Evening School in Colonial America.** 1925.

Seybolt, Robert Francis. **Source Studies in American Colonial Education.** 1925.

Todd, Lewis Paul. **Wartime Relations of the Federal Government and the Public Schools, 1917-1918.** 1945.

Vandewalker, Nina C. **The Kindergarten in American Education.** 1908.

Ward, Florence Elizabeth. **The Montessori Method and the American School.** 1913.

West, Andrew Fleming. **Short Papers on American Liberal Education.** 1907.

Wright, Marion M. Thompson. **The Education of Negroes in New Jersey.** 1941.

Supplement

The Social Frontier (Frontiers of Democracy). Vols. 1-10, 1934-1943.